ANOTHER LITTLE HORN

A Study of the U.S. in Prophecy

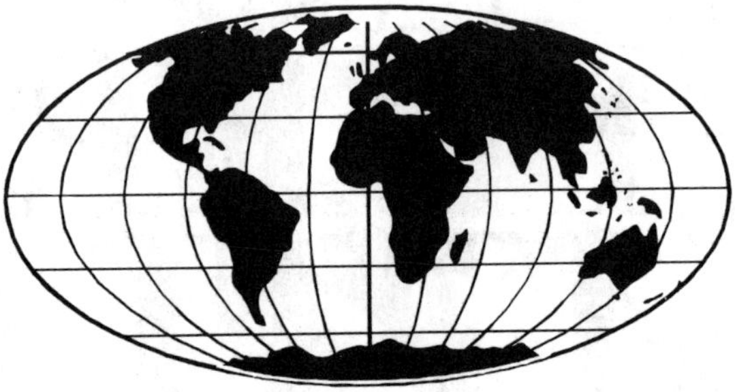

Another Little Horn
A Study of the U.S. in Prophecy

John R. Broyles

Alpha **Ω** *mega Press*
Vass, North Carolina 28394

© 1995 by John R. Broyles

Published by Alpha-Omega Press
154 Creekbend, Vass, NC 28394

Printed in the United States of America

All rights reserved. No part of this publication may be reproduced, stored in a retrieval system, or transmitted in any form or by any means - electronic, mechanical, photocopy, recording, or any other - without the prior written permission of the publisher. The only exception is brief quotes in printed reviews.

Broyles, John R.
  Another Little Horn

Christian non-fiction, American.
ISBN: 0-9645494-3-3

Scripture taken from the HOLY BIBLE, King James Version.

Contents Ω

	Foreword by Rev. Charles R. Grisham	*vii*
	Author's Note	*viii*
	Preface	*ix*
1	Nebuchadnezzar's Dream	1
2	Beasts Out of the Sea	9
3	And It Had Ten Horns	21
4	The Identity of the Ten Horns	27
5	Another Little Horn	40
6	Plucked Up by the Roots	46
7	The Eyes of Man	53
8	A Mouth Speaking Great Things	58
9	The Spirit of America	63
10	Jesus is Coming	72
11	Made War With the Saints	76
12	Change	100
13	The Ancient of Days	108
14	A Time, Times, and the Dividing of Times	112
15	Like Unto a Leopard	127
16	Freedom	141
17	More Amazing Faith	154
	Epilogue	164
	Bibliography	165

Acknowledgements

Unending thankfulness to God for His mercy and grace to me in completion of this work.

Special recognition to my sister, Marjorie Kinnee, for countless hours spent in computerizing, proof reading, typesetting, artistry and promoting the work.

Honor to my great friend, Charles Grisham, for writing the foreword and many years of support and friendship in life's trying hours.

Honor to my late father, John Sr. (known to his friends as "Ray"), and to my mother, Marjorie, for years of steadfast Christian upbringing.

Recognition and honor to all the pastors in my life; C.C. Kirby, C.G. Kirby, Carl Hill, Terry Crosby, Stanley Wilt and Jeff Chavis.

Recommendation of the "Lincoln Library" to all readers. It was the source of many dates and historical facts. I have spent many hours with this enjoyable reference work since I was eight years old.

Foreword

It is an honor and a unique pleasure to introduce to you this book by my friend, John Broyles. **"Another Little Horn"** addresses things that are as current as tomorrow's headlines while reminding us of the ancient prophecies which earlier seemed far away.

The contents of this scholarly work will enable you to become more alert to current developments in the light of where we are as a church. We need to be awake and aware so we may allow God's Word to guide us through the most critical time we have ever known.

Bro. John Broyles has been a personal friend for many years. I have found him to be a humble servant of God, a lover of souls and a student of God's Word.

At this present time he has a burden for the lost masses of the nation of Turkey and a vision of a mighty Holy Ghost outpouring in the Mideast. He recently returned from spending three months in Turkey laying prayerful groundwork and has plans to return and continue in '95. Any proceeds from this book will greatly help in fulfilling this dream.

So as you read, keep your Bible and notepad handy. You will come away informed and challenged to do more to spread this glorious Gospel.

Yours in Christ,

Charles R. Grisham, Pastor
New Life Apostolic Church
Detroit, Michigan

Author's Note

The United States of America is the spirit and embodiment of the "little horn" of Daniel, chapter seven. Those who love America and everything it represents may may strongly resent the message contained in these pages. For this, I cannot apologize.

As a citizen, I fully appreciate the advantages of living in American society. As a minister of the gospel, I must condemn the sinfulness of that same social system.

As a lover of prophecy and history, I have spent some ten years researching, writing, analyzing, and rewriting this work. My goal is to foster an understanding of the times in which we live. I also want to inspire a thirst for knowledge of God in both myself and in each reader - beyond that which we have presently achieved.

John R. Broyles

Preface

The heart of every knowledgable person in America deplores the direction this nation is taking. People who love righteousness cannot reconcile the love of country we have been taught with the abortion, crime, hate, adultery, homosexuality and evil lifestyles emanating from and permeating our society. Everything is not all sweetness and light when it comes to this great America the Beautiful, home of the fruited plain.

There is a ragged knife edge of wickedness in this nation that cuts up innocent unborn babies and boils their little bodies down into anti-wrinkle cream - an evil product for older women to rub on their faces, hoping for another night of sinfulness. There is something badly wrong in a country where even the little children are selling drugs and murdering their customers - and where their own mothers and brothers and sisters are the customers!

Television and the airwaves in America are filled with moral sewage. Every imaginable evil thing is paraded for all to see and emulate. America the Beautiful has gone to the dogs and much worse things are just around the corner. It's time for people to wake up and realize why...

The Star Spangled Banner

Oh say can you see,
By the dawn's early light;
What so proudly we hailed,
At the twilight's last gleaming;
Whose broad stripes and bright stars,
Through the perilous night,
O'er the ramparts we watched,
Were so gallantly streaming.
And the rocket's red glare,
The bombs bursting in air,
Gave proof through the night,
That our flag was still there.
Oh say, does that
Star-spangled banner yet wave;
O'er the land of the free,
And the home of the brave?

The Continental United States of America

Chapter I
Nebuchadnezzar's Dream

"I considered the horns, and behold, there came up among them another little horn..." (Daniel 7:8).

The United States of America is the "little horn" described in Daniel chapter seven. Daniel was the greatest apocalyptic prophet of the Hebrew Old Testament. About the year 555 B.C., God began to show Daniel through dreams and visions a grievous and troublesome picture of things to come. In these visions and dreams, human government on a world-wide scale was revealed to Daniel as resembling a series of great and dreadful beasts. They were terrible in nature;

devouring and breaking, dominating and destroying like wild beasts in the earth. The fourth beast, diverse from the others and "exceeding dreadful," was identified as having ten horns on his head.

> *"I considered the horns, and, behold, there came up among them another little horn, before whom there were three of the first horns plucked up by the roots: and, behold, in this horn were eyes like the eyes of a man, and a mouth speaking great things."*   *(Daniel 7:8)*

Nebuchadnezzar's Dream

God's purpose in the creation of earth's system is to reveal Himself to man on an individual basis. God, for His own reasons, created a world in which man is dominant over the other creatures. He also gave us free agency. We are free to choose our own way in this world (but of course we have to pay the price for our choices). Yet everything we do and all we experience leads us inexorably toward the awareness and recognition of the existence of God. What we do with that knowledge is also up to us as individuals. God is looking for people who will still make the right choices. No matter what our choices might be, whether to our credit or not, God is going to get the glory. Everyone who ever existed is sooner or later going to come to the firsthand knowledge of the awesome power and greatness of our Lord and Savior, Jesus Christ.

God began to reveal, even in Daniel's time, the nature

and identity of the various forms of the kingdoms of this world. As early as 603 B.C., Nebuchadnezzar, king of the Babylonian system, had a great and mysterious dream from God interpreted for him by the prophet Daniel (Daniel 2). In this dream, Nebuchadnezzar saw human government on the earth as a huge metal image of a man. The head of this image was fine gold. The chest and arms were of silver. The belly and thighs were of brass. The legs were made of iron and the feet of iron mixed with clay. As the king watched, a great stone cut out without hands smote the image on its feet of clay and the entire image was destroyed. The stone, meanwhile, became a great mountain and filled the whole earth (Daniel 2:31-45).

Daniel told Nebuchadnezzar that he and his Babylonian kingdom were this head of gold. Gold represents the zenith of value in metals. It is pure in nature, does not tarnish with age, is much sought after and is rare and very costly. The Babylonian kingdom was identified as golden because of its pureness of form. The king was absolute ruler in Babylon. There was no higher or equal power. There was no amelioration of his rule. Whatever the king decreed was absolute. He could explore to the fullest extent every avenue of his desires. He could change his mind if he wished and reverse direction. But there was no running to mama 'cause daddy said no.

The king ordered the furnace heated seven times hotter than usual and the three Hebrew children thrown into it (Daniel 3:21-22), and that is exactly what took place. The king's rule was so strong and his command so urgent that several of his strongest men perished from the heat of the furnace while throwing the Hebrews into it.

Prophetic scholars have concluded that God likened the Babylonian kingdom to gold because it is the most desirable system of government. God Himself rules His Kingdom in this way. God is approachable and can be influenced but His rule is absolute. Human systems are limited by the inadequacies and faults of leadership; however, God is without fault or inadequacy. He is not limited in His ways. Moreover, God is inherently good. Therefore, His leadership is good in every way.

Bible scholars and historians alike have long identified the second kingdom in Nebuchadnezzar's dream with the Medo-Persian empire. It dominated the ancient world from 538 B.C. to 334 B.C. This is what Nebuchadnezzar saw as the breast and arms of silver. The Medo-Persian empire, like all four empires in this prophecy, had conquered or at least was capable of conquering the known world of that time. In particular, they all ruled the area of the city of Jerusalem. This is the city of God (Psalm 46:4), the joy of the whole earth (Psalm 48:2), the perfection of beauty (Lamentations 2:15), and the city of our solemnities (Isaiah 33:20).

The fundamental difference between the Babylonians and the Medo-Persians was the concept of the rule of law. In the Medo-Persian empire, the king was no longer absolute. He was bound by his own word. When the king issued a decree, as when Darius was induced to ban all prayer to any God or man save the king, the law of the Medes and the Persians was such that no decree of the king could be changed (Daniel 6:15). When Daniel violated the decree by praying to God, even the king himself could not save Daniel from the lions.

In contrast, the God of Heaven is not limited in any way. He certainly is not limited by His own Word (contrary to what some might think). Jonah was certainly uttering the word of the Lord when he preached, *"Yet forty days and Ninevah shall be overthrown." (Jonah 3:4)*. Yet God was not limited by His own word to Jonah, for when Ninevah repented of their evil ways, God also repented of the evil He said He would do unto them. If God was limited and bound by His own word, then Ninevah would have been immediately destroyed. If God was limited and bound by His own word, then the Old Testament could never have been superseded by the New. We know His Word is true. We also need to know that God is absolutely unlimited in every way.

The third kingdom in Nebuchadnezzar's dream was represented by the belly and thighs of brass. Biblical historians recognize this as the Grecian empire, which was personified by Alexander the Great, the most notable conqueror of the ancient world. The Grecian empire held sway from about 334 B.C. to 136 B.C. and was the first to dominate the culture and politics of all three continents of the civilizations of antiquity. The Greeks colonized widespread portions of western Europe and the near east. The conquering armies of Alexander marched from Africa to India and through vast stretches of Asia. Everywhere they went, the Greeks left indelible marks of their culture. Government, language, literature, architecture, medicine, mathematics, science and warfare were all revolutionized by their vigorousness. The Greeks introduced the ideas of democracy and philosophy. While their dominion has long since dissipated, it can yet be said that the golden age of

Greece still spans the globe.

The fourth kingdom in Nebuchadnezzar's dream was the Roman empire, represented by the legs of iron and feet made of iron mixed with clay. Rome came to world power about 146 B.C., succeeding the Greeks and the general anarchy left by the gradual decay of their empire. Just like the two legs of Nebuchadnezzar's image, Rome was divided into two halves, eastern and western, each with its own capital city and divergent culture. This division, begun by the emperor Constantine in 330 A.D., led to more far-reaching results than he had ever anticipated. The Roman empire had become the strongest the world had ever seen, but the two halves drifted farther and farther apart socially and politically. Each half was under great pressure from barbarians who came from the fringes of the empire. Both the East and the West eventually folded before these pressures, though at different times. This mutual event has been heralded as the decline and/or fall of the Roman Empire.

Modern day evangelical scholars have consistently and (rarely for them) universally looked on these political defeats as being the end of the Roman empire per se. They have taught that there will be a revival of the Roman empire under the antichrist during the time known as "Jacob's trouble" or the "tribulation" in prophetic terms. It might be said that this is a form of a lowest common denominator prophetically. Many events associated with "tribulation," the "antichrist" and the "mark of the beast" are spoken of in Bible prophecy, but the Lord also said "that at evening time it shall be light" (Zechariah 14:7). More and more things are becoming apparent to us as the evening progresses.

It might be noticed here that Nebuchadnezzar's image was not cut off at the knees. One of the keys to understanding the book of Daniel lies in the feet of the image. In the latter days of this kingdom (progressing from head to toe) they shall mingle themselves with the seed of men (Daniel 2:43).

Look at the nations that bear the heritage of the old Roman empire. One or two hundred years ago you could look at Italy and it would have been full of Italians, Spain with Spaniards, Britain with Britishers and so forth. But today Germany is full of Turks and Kurds and Bosnians. France is full of Algerians and Africans. England is full of Jamaicans, Pakistanis, Sri Lankans, and what have you, but they do not cleave one to another. Turks riot in Germany, unhappy Algerians demonstrate in France, and on and on it goes.

The strength of iron is still in these nations. Look at what the allied nations did to Iraq in the Persian Gulf war. They purely stomped on Saddam Hussein and then they went in after the war and broke up and bulldozed his chemical weapons and giant cannons, etc. Old Titus Flavius Vespasian couldn't have done it any better. This was quintessential Roman empire.

Saddam Hussein &
President George Bush

But just a few years later, look at what these modern day wonders did in Somalia. They bumbled and stumbled. A bunch of ragtag, half-starved urchins and assorted street wretches put to flight the best troops the world had to offer. It was not by defeating them in battle but by defeating them nonetheless: partly strong and partly broken.

We need to realize that none of these entities have ceased to exist. The Roman empire is still with us today. These things cannot just be swept under the rug; neither history's rug, nor tribulation's rug. The current events unfolding before our very eyes have everything to do with Bible prophecy.

New York City Skyline:
America's cultural heritage and foundations
are derived from the European Nations.

Chapter II
Beasts Out of the Sea

Nebuchadnezzar may have been king, but he was no spiritual giant. His dream (in chapter two) came through human perspective; but in chapter seven, we find Daniel seeing things on a spiritual level.

In Daniel's vision, the four winds of heaven strove upon the great sea. Four great beasts came up from the sea which represents the masses of humanity. The beasts seen here are again the four great world powers; Babylon, Medo-Persia, Greece and Rome; the same ones seen in Nebuchadnezzar's dream. Daniel saw them as beasts because that is their true nature. When we look back into history at all the violence, the blood and gore that have been caused by the wars of these nations (and the associated pillage, rapine and plundering) we can understand why they are called beasts. It is when men gang together that their worst behavior is brought out. Then they do things they would never have thought of on their own.

The four winds of heaven, which are mentioned numerous times throughout Scripture, represent the striving of various characteristics in the national make-up of these empires. The east wind in Scripture is characterized as vehement and blasting (Genesis 41:6; Jonah 4:8). The west wind is a strong wind that brings showers. The north wind drives away rain, while the south wind brings heat and causes the spices to grow.

Every aspect of these empires is beastly. There is an unreasoning wildness associated with their beastliness. A pack of wild dogs may break in on a flock of sheep and kill or maim every one of them without hardly taking a bite of the meat. This is the beastly nature in them, compounded by the powerful spirit of the pack. Unless proper care is taken, a flock of turkeys in a poultry house may panic and all pile up in one corner of the building, smothering and crushing themselves to death in great numbers - their wild instinct compounded by great numbers. Wild fans will do the same thing at a soccer stadium or a rock concert. When great masses of people come together in a wild way like this, they do things they would never do on their own - like trample each other to death. The sum of the whole is greater than the sum of the individual parts.

This greedy, wild beast behavior is the thing that

makes a nation dissatisfied with merely mining things out of the ground. They are driven to strip mine and leave the earth ruined and desolate behind them. This is the cause of polluted rivers, lakes and oceans. This is the rationale behind the toxic waste dumps across the land. This wild "beastialism" is causing men to prepare (dig up) nuclear destruction for themselves, that they might die before their time.

Each of these world empires were characterized by such bestial behavior. None of the four came to power by genteel methods and reasonableness and their power was and is sustained by violence, war, intrigue and intimidation. Let us look at these powers as Daniel saw them.

Babylon

The first beast was like a lion and had eagle's wings. This, as we have previously mentioned, is the Babylonian empire under Nebuchadnezzar and his successors.

One of the most important concepts to visualize and build upon concerning the Gentile world powers is the basic difference between spiritual realities and the embodiment of that spirit. Saint John gave us many details concerning the coming of the antichrist during the time of the tribulation. The book of Revelation reveals many details. Yet, in his first epistle, John stated plainly that the spirit of antichrist was already working in the world (two thousand years ago). Not having a body yet, the spirit of antichrist has been busy all this time, working toward the deception of the nations. So, when we begin to consider an entity like the Babylonian empire, there is more to it all than just a sand-choked city of mud, bricks and a few years of ancient history.

Babylon had its start in antiquity right after the flood of Noah's day - at the Tower of Babel. In contravention of the commandments of God, man built a tower to withstand another mighty flood (which God had promised would not occur,) and to make a name for themselves. Their purpose was confounded by God, Himself.

Daniel saw a beast like a lion which had eagle's wings. The lion has often been characterized as the king of beasts. Solomon noted that the lion *"turneth not away for any." (Proverbs 30:30)*. Add to this the wings of an eagle and we find an empire of noble strength travelling the highways of humanity which had not been previously experienced. Babylon was the first of the ancient Holy Land conquering empires that in its glory days knew no rival capable of withstanding its power. Yet those glory days were soon over. Daniel noted four things which followed:

1. The eagle's wings were plucked,
2. It was lifted up from the earth,
3. It was made to stand upon the feet of a man,
4. A man's heart was given to it.

After its defeat and absorption into the Medo-Persian empire, Babylon no longer went with eagle's wings; nor did its successors attain that ability. Of all the Gentile world powers, it was only the Babylonians, Nebuchadnezzar and Belshazzar (in the "plucked" sense,) who obtained understanding in the highways of spiritual wisdom. What other heathen king had a whole chapter of the Bible to himself to address all the saints throughout history? Thus, the eagle's wings.

After its defeat, the Babylonian way was not left to

decay as did other great powers. The Babylonians are not known to us by their tombs, as the Egyptians or the ancient Chinese. Rather, the Babylonian way has taken on an aura of mystique which is elevated above common earthiness. There is a Babylonian spirit which is both ancient and yet prevalent in the world today.

The Babylonian spirit stands on its feet like a man. It is no longer going about this world as a beast, doing incomprehensible things. What we see instead is a spirit of anything goes multi-culturalism. The Babel that started in Nimrod's tower has been changed into something profound. There is a human heart to this thing; one that transcends the ways of antiquity.

Medo-Persia

The second beast Daniel saw was likened unto a bear. We have already noted the Medo-Persian empire as the embodiment of a bear. It was raised up on one side due to the dominant Persian influence in this union. Like a bear, the Medo-Persians came to power by prowling ways. They prowled around the city of Babylon until they found a way to divert the Euphrates River, which flowed via a massive gate right through the heart of Babylon. They entered the city by night through the now-dry river bed and captured the kingdom.

Like a bear, the Medo-Persians were constantly hungry and on the go. They exhibited a voracious appetite for land and peoples which brought them an empire stretching from India to Egypt. But their government and armies, while huge and powerful, were also clumsy and inefficient. When an insatiable appetite for more led Darius III to invade and attack the Greek armies of Alexander the Great, it proved to be their undoing. The Medo-Persian empire collapsed before the vigor of a Greek onslaught they could not resist.

Much like the Babylonians, the spiritual nature of the Medo-Persian empire is still with us today. Daniel said their lives were preserved for a time but their dominion was taken away.

Greece

The third beast Daniel saw was likened unto a leopard. It had four wings of a fowl and four heads. The leopard, known for swiftness combined with strength and agility, is symbolic of the Grecian empire (334-146 B.C.). It took Alexander the Great just eight years to conquer the ancient world from Europe to Egypt to the Indus River. He accomplished this magnitude of success at the head of a small army (equal to three American divisions). These were dedicated men of special spirit.

Robin Fox's book, "The Search for Alexander", (Little, Brown & Co.) provides an excellent account of the Greek exploits. In the Battle of Gaugamela alone, Persian casualties were estimated to be as high as 300,000 men. How did such a relatively small force triumph so spectacularly in battles which were fought eyeball to eyeball, sword against sword, and shield against shield?

The answer lies in the almost worshipful awe and loyalty exhibited by Alexander's men. He had a tremendous personal charisma and readily knew how to use it. This character combination is a highly effective motivator of men, especially in military endeavors. General George McClellan (Union - Civil War) had it.

Napoleon had it; but none of these were as effective as Alexander.

He probably hastened his own death by getting up too early from a grievous arrow wound sustained in the Indian campaign. Persistent rumors had spread among the troops that he had died. So when he appeared riding a horse among them shortly thereafter, the motivational affect was astounding. For leadership of this type, men will attempt almost anything and their success rate will be very high.

In Daniel's vision we find the Grecian empire depicted as having the four wings of a fowl on its back; showing that in a symbolic sense, the Greeks could fly above the ordinary ways of mankind. These were not the wings of an eagle (like Nebuchadnezzar's Babylonians) but they were wings nevertheless. This explains the extraordinary legacy the Greeks left in the arts and sciences. Consider this short list of names; Plato, Socrates, Pythagoras, Pericles, Archimedes and Herodotus (the list could go on and on); history, philosophy, higher mathematics, medicine... In many ways the Greeks flew above their fellows.

Yet, however great a man might become and however great a nation might be, we need to keep things in perspective. When the creature is great, look to the Creator. When the spectacle is awesome, thank God for giving you the eyes to see it.

The Grecian empire had four heads. Upon the death of Alexander at the early age of thirty two, his empire broke into four parts (headed by his leading generals). Feuding amongst themselves along the way, the Greeks still managed to hold dominion in their empire for nearly two hundred years before finally giving way to the rising

Roman empire. This may be dated to 146 B.C., when The last vestiges of Greek power were overwhelmed by the Roman legions.

Rome

Daniel saw *"a fourth beast, dreadful and terrible, and strong exceedingly..." (Daniel 7:7).*

The Roman empire has been much examined by a number of prophetic scholars and by historians galore. We are not so much interested here in the history of Rome as in how we are affected by it. What influence does the Roman empire have on us today?

The central authority of the empire is not what it used to be, of course; but the member states (horns or provinces) are very much intact. In history (since the purported "fall") we find periods of time in which individual nations among the ten have held a vestige of imperial power. Napoleon, Hitler, the Hapsburgs, the "Holy Roman" emperors and others have, as virtual emperors, practically controlled the land area. We also see the approaching political embodiment of the Common Market developing into something that is just a step away from full restoration of the empire. Additionally, there have been considerable periods in history in which the Vatican has virtually controlled continental politics. So while there may not have always been a titled emperor (the Holy Roman Emperor was titled) there has not always been a power vacuum either.

Man's way is to look on things with the natural eyes. He sees ancient Rome as a large, heroic conquering government. The Romans erected great quantities of impressive stone architecture, some of which is still with us today. The Colosseum, the aqueducts and the Roman roads; these are not the kinds of legacies that lead people to think ill of them. A system that efficiently ruled the world's commerce for six hundred years is viewed with great respect (and not aversion) by most people. When thinking about the Roman political and military systems, its glory stands out. But looks can be deceiving.

The Romans had another face that was not so glorious. Their Colosseum was a sports palace in which the major sport was watching people kill one another by various entertaining methods. Some were given weapons and sent to kill each other. Some were set on by lions or other wild beasts and chewed or mauled to death for the crowd's amusement. Many entertaining methods of slaughtering the victims were devised and thousands of people flocked to the games. It was all great fun for them and became so popular that many provincial stadiums were erected across the empire for the same purpose.

When Caesar came to watch the games, the gladiators who fought were induced to greet him saying: "We who are about to die salute you."

When the Romans fought a war and won, they very often took the vanquished foes to slavery in the mines. Many others were condemned to participation in these "games." Josephus narrates the following concerning the taking of Jerusalem in 74 A.D.:

"And now since his soldiers were already quite tired of killing men, and yet there appeared to be a vast multitude still remaining alive, Caesar gave orders that they should kill none but those that were in arms and opposed them, but should take the rest alive. But together with those whom they had orders to slay, they slew the aged and infirm; but for those who were in their flourishing age ... Fronto slew all those who had been seditious and robbers, who were impeached by one another; but of the young men he chose out the tallest ad most beautiful and reserved them for the triumph; and as for the rest of the multitude that were above seventeen years old, he put them into bonds and sent them into the Egyptian mines. Titus also sent a great number into the provinces, as a present to them, that they might be destroyed upon their theaters, by the sword and by wild beasts; but those under seventeen years of age were sold as slaves.

Now the number of those that were carried captive during this whole war was collected to be ninety seven thousand; as was the number of those that perished during the whole siege eleven hundred thousand..."[1]

So they took 97,000 captives, who were for the most part doomed, and 1.1 million people were put directly to death. This immense cruelty is typical of what the Romans inflicted. People who acquiesced to their harsh system suffered greatly, but those who resisted were absolutely annihilated.

The death by crucifixion which Jesus suffered was a common method of Roman execution. The idea was to inflict as much pain as possible. Hands and feet were nailed to a cross, tree or wooden post (In itself this is not a mortal wound.). The victim's weight was supported on the nails in his hands unless he could push his feet against the nails pinning them to the wood block below. It was excruciatingly painful. It could be said that the

---

[1] The Works of Flavius Josephus (Baker Book House, 1979), vol. 1, pp. 468-9.

cause of death was agony. To hasten the death of the two thieves crucified with Jesus, the soldiers broke their legs, which meant they couldn't push up any more to catch their breath or relieve the pressure on their hands and arms. This was something less than a favor.

Some have said that the hand-wounds the Lord suffered must have been in His wrists because the hand could not have carried the weight. This shows how far removed our culture is from painful reality.

The Romans seemed to delight in this sort of cruelty. In the siege at Jerusalem in 70 A.D., they grew weary of the fact that not many Jews were accepting their offer of amnesty. So they began crucifying everyone they could get their hands on, particularly those found trying to slip through the lines to safety. Soon they had the roadside lined with crosses. Estimates have put the number of Jews killed this way at 50,000.

Behavior of this sort is not humane by any standard. It is beastly; but also typical of the way the Romans operated - a system the like of which the world had never seen.

Of course this is first grade stuff. Cruelty is nothing new and was not new in that day either. But the Romans were efficient like no one had ever been before. Their methods produced what they called the "Pax Romana;" (the Roman peace). This was a time of generalized peace and safety, particularly for the central and more populated portions of the empire. It lasted hundreds of years and created a great climate for business. Merchants and others who grew fat by exploiting it were highly appreciative. But the "Pax Romana" was generated by policies of utter brutality. Daniel spoke of how the beast *"devoured and brake in pieces, and stamped the residue with the feet of it." (Daniel 7:7).*

Consider the fate of the Carthagenians. They signed a peace treaty with Rome and were adhering to it themselves. But the Romans would have none of it. Due to an intense political hatred, they came back in, either killed or put to slavery the inhabitants, tore the city to the ground, plowed the ground up and then sowed salt into the ground to make it incapable of agriculture.

Much the same thing was done to Jerusalem after it fell to Titus in 70 A.D. Simon, son of Gioras, one of the principal leaders of the Jewish revolt, went into hiding in an underground cave below the temple complex. Several weeks later he came up to make good his escape, only to find himself in the middle of a plowed field. The Romans had removed every stone from that particular place, much to the astonishment of Simon, who was then left to the tender mercies of his Roman captors.

The Statue of Liberty:
A gift to the American People from the Nation of France.

Chapter III
And It Had Ten Horns

Much of current eschatology is based on the premise that the Roman empire died in 500 A.D. or so and will be evilly and miraculously revived during the tribulation with some combination of ten of the Common Market nations. It is important to remember however, that Nebuchadnezzar's image was not **cut off** at the knees (or the ankles either, for that matter). The Vandals and Goths who sacked Rome were themselves part of the empire (an unruly part, it's true) and had been for years.

These events heralded a turning point as far as central authority was concerned, but this so-called central authority of the empire was at best fragmented already. Its command of the empire had been only sporadic for years. Julius Caesar's assassination in 44 B.C. demonstrates that power struggles have always been a part of the foundation of the Roman Empire.

Note Daniel 7:17 and compare it with Daniel 7:24:

Daniel 7:17	Daniel 7:24
*"These great beasts, which are four, are four **kings** which shall arise out of the earth."*	*"And the ten horns out of this kingdom are ten **kings** that shall arise: and another shall rise after them; and he shall be diverse from the first, and he shall subdue three **kings**."*

Key in on the word "kings." In both cases they are the same Hebrew and Aramaic word, "melek" (4430, Strongs). Now, we know that the four kings referred to in verse 17 are not just kings, although there may have been a central figurehead (i.e. Nebuchadnezzar), but these are kingdoms and empires. Verse 24 uses the same word, kings, to describe the ten kings which are the ten horns of the terrible beast. These are not just the ten toes which arise in tribulation (although there will be ten toes during the tribulation). These ten horns are in the **head** of the beast as well. We are talking about a head to toe vision here.

The problem in identifying prophetic imagery is threefold. First is the principle of light at evening time. Some things were not capable of being understood years ago because the time was not right. Secondly, there is at times, a failure in dividing the scriptures rightly. Each portion of prophetic scripture both has its own individual application and also needs to be properly meshed together with other portions. Thirdly, if the foundation is misdirected, anything built upon it is subject to go astray.

Some have accepted ideas put out by secular sources, such as Gibbons' "Decline and Fall of the Roman Empire," as being inerrant and incorporate them right into their theology.

Without doubt, Gibbons researched his **facts** in great detail, but his major premise - the decline and fall of the Roman Empire - is both premature and misses the prophetic point; namely - the continued existence of the Roman Empire per se. If good and well-meaning Christians rely on misdirected or deceptive concepts, they will have an awfully rough time getting past the untruth or half truth they have believed, to see the real truth later on. No doubt, this is Satan's intention in the first place when he leads well meaning people astray. But we are not ignorant of his devices.

Some scholars have made an intense study of the Word of God but don't know the God of the Word. What good does it do to study but then teach the commandments of men over those of God? When a man gets to be such an expert that he will turn out his own annotated version of the scriptures - where his comments fill up the page and the word of God is left to a few lines per page - we need to begin taking his teachings with a grain of salt. We cannot accept verbatim the teachings of the scholars of renown. We must search the scriptures to see whether these things are so.

"The ten horns ... are ten kings that shall arise..." (Daniel 7:24). This refers to the ten nations arising out of the Roman Empire. We have to be cautious about slapping labels on here because the scripture does not (for the most part) identify the ten individually. We know they are all indigenous parts of the Roman empire and take their rise from it. We also know they are all kings in the same context that Babylon, Medo-Persia, Greece and Rome are kings. Therefore, they have all exercised a measure of dominion within the confines of the old Roman system. What we are looking for is going to have:

1.) a sense of national identity,
2.) a common language or in some cases a common ethnicity or spirit that unites
two or more different cultures, and
3.) nations that at some point in their history have become a dominant force, controlling substantial portions of the old Roman empire.

We recognize that the Roman empire split into an eastern and a western segment. This is the two legs of iron. We must also realize that there is both an embodiment and a spiritual nature to these nations and that the spiritual legs are oriented differently than the carnal ones.

Since the time that the emperor, Constantine "converted" to Christianity, a religious entity has been involved here. While the secular authority of the eastern and Western empires was slipping away, there was a corresponding rise in the temporal powers of the popes or "bishops" of Rome in the west and or the patriarch of the Eastern Orthodox churches in the east. However, this work will not be delving into religious history.

One important thing to consider here is the Muslim states (Arabian conquests) and the Ottoman empire. Both of these related groups have exercised control over substantial portions of the old Roman empire for a great period of time. However, it is important to realize here, that their coverage and control of the land and the people is (borrowing from the terminology of George Bush's popularity,) a mile wide and an inch deep.

Anyone familiar with Turkey, for example, knows that while the mosques are huge, attendance is small. The whole population is unified in an intense longing for things secular and western. The myth of a popular-based resurgence of Muslim fundamentalism is just that - a myth - fostered in Iran and perpetuated in spite of demographic facts by a fickle, sensation mongering press. There are a number of fanatics but they get an inordinate amount of press time.

It must be remembered that all through the periods of Muslim conquest there has been a recurrent and persistent underlying thread of Roman empire revivalism and recidivism (a tendency to relapse into Roman empire-type behavior). Consider the fact that the Asian Constantinople based empire was not dislodged until 1453 A.D. The European (and Romanly vicious) crusaders held substantial portions of the Holy Land from 1099 until 1270 A.D. Additionally, the European nations of Britain, France and Italy held colonial control over Iraq, Iran, Jordan, Syria, Palestine, Egypt, the Sudan and the entirety of Muslim North Africa for one hundred and fifty years prior to World War II. So, the Muslim control in these areas has not been monolithic.

World class military power is not based in the windswept sand barrens of Arabia and Persia. The reference in Revelation 16:12 to the drying up of the River Euphrates to prepare the way of the kings of the east does **not** refer to Turkey's upstream dam, not to the physical aspects of water at all. A river such as the Euphrates is not a serious obstacle to a modern army. Were it so, the Indus and the Ganges would have to dry up as well. Rather, Revelation 16:12 is a reference to a national withering of the vitality of the associated states in this region. What happened to Saddam Hussein is a prime example.

Rhinoceros

Chapter IV
The Identity of the Ten Horns

In the animal kingdom, horns are for one purpose - to push with: to get violent, to thrust out rivals or enemies, to drive them out, etc. Consider how a rhinoceros uses its horn, or a he-goat, bull, ram, or buck deer. Their horns are used to push their competition and all interlopers around with; for territorial and/or domination purposes.

So when we look back in history for the identities of the ten horns, we are going to see two special characteristics. There will be a rooted connection to the old Roman empire. We will also see that there has been a lot of pushing going on whenever one of these horns arises. It's rather like babies teething. When the horns start rising, the nation gets irritable and cranky. It starts making a big fuss and poking people with its horn. So in history we look for a time of rapid expansion, military conquest and the push of intense economic activity; all emanating from the national source of the horn. Of course some people are going to get poked - or perhaps gored and trampled to death.

We find the following characteristics common among the ten "horn" nations:

COMMON CHARACTERISTICS of the "HORN" NATIONS
1. All trace their roots to the old Roman empire.
2. All ten are of Caucasian origin (Japheth).
3. All ten have arisen to substantial military/economic power and influence at one or more points since 146 B.C.
4. All have mingled themselves with peoples of diverse ethnic backgrounds.
5. All are in national decline - (the glory years are over).

It is important not to let the clouds of current events obscure our view of the facts. Contemporary press/journalism is highly colored by the spirits and prejudices of the age. Fuller understanding is not going to be facilitated by the type of data the evening news programs and newspapers are putting out.

The ten horns of Daniel's fourth beast (the Roman empire) are as follows:

1. Italy (Rome)
2. Spain
3. Portugal
4. France/Belgium
5. Great Britain
6. The Netherlands
7. Germany
8. Austria-Hungary
9. Russia (Slavic Nations)
10. Anatolia (Constantinople, Asia or Turkey)

Each of these ten "horn nations" can be identified by the five horn nation characteristics noted previously. We need to include a brief synopsis of the nature of each of these ten nations. This information is based primarily on historical data guided by the principles set forth by the prophet Daniel.

We might begin by noting those several Roman connected nations which are **not** among the ten horn nations.

1. Greece
2. Persia (Iran)
3. Babylonia (Iraq)
4. Assyria
5. Egypt

Greece, Persia and Babylonia are not included due to Daniel's explanation in Chapter 7, verse 12. While conquered by Rome, these are exempt from horn status. They have not exhibited dominion over the other nations in any way since they were overthrown, but their lives have been prolonged.

Assyria and Egypt (together with the first three) represent the remaining five fallen kings of Revelation 17:10. Though they were Roman provinces, their dominion is also in the past (Rome is the sixth and of the other two we cannot speak as yet).

The Ten Horn Nations of Rome

1. Italy

The home of Rome and the wellspring of the Roman empire. From beginnings as early as 750 B.C., the Italian nation reached the height of its power in the dimensions of the early empire (circa 180 A.D.). Existing in a mostly fragmented condition for thirteen hundred years, Italy saw revitalization in the nineteenth century. Colonialism was revived and overseas possessions included Libya, Ethiopia, Albania and Eritrea. Modern Italian adventurism in the person of Benito Mussolini was subdued by the United States, aided by the British, in 1943 (World War II).

2. Spain

Conquered by Rome around 200 B.C., Spain endured numerous lengthy periods of national subjugation until the late fifteenth century. At that time King Ferdinand and Queen Isabella united the nation and began an incredible push of world-wide dimensions. Beginning with the exploits of Christopher Columbus in 1492, Spain seized colonial possessions that included most of South and Central America, Mexico, California, Florida and great portions of the American west. Added to this were territories in northwest Africa, the Philippines and far-flung possessions in the isles of the seas.

But Spanish adventurism was not equalled by Spanish administration. Beginning with Columbus, the success of Spanish governing left something to be desired. One by one, Spain's great overseas possessions fell by the wayside until the last bastions of Spanish power were taken by the United States following the Spanish-American conflict in 1898. Spain has shown a subdued face to the world for the most part since that war, remaining neutral in both World Wars and taking no vigorous political positions internationally.

3. Portugal

Populated by a people known as Lusitanians, Portugal fought the Romans vigorously prior to the first century B.C., but eventually were conquered. The Portuguese came to power in the person of Henry the Navigator in the early fifteenth century. The Portuguese Man-o-war is a jelly-fish like creature of the seas that sensible seafarers soon learn to leave alone. Its name and reputation stem from the similar attributes of Portugal's intrepid seafarers. During the colonial era, Portugal controlled the entire nation of Brazil, portions of India, plus the Azores Islands, Indonesia, the Cape Verde Islands, Morocco, and the Guinea Coast. Portugal entered World War I on the side of the allies but remained neutral throughout World War II.

4. France (and Belgium)

The present day nation of Belgium was a portion of the larger Roman province of Gallia Belgica. Conquered and added to the Roman empire by Julius Caesar in 58 B.C., France has enjoyed considerable success as the western strength of the European continent. French colonialism brought extensive possessions in central North America, French West Africa, China, Indochina, Syria, Algeria, Senegal and many others. The French colonial area at the turn of the twentieth century was twenty times larger than the national homeland. Overrun by the Nazi Germans in World War II, occupied France was liberated by the allied invasions of 1944 and today has regained a position of considerable military strength in Europe.

5. Great Britain

The Romans established themselves in south Britain in the invasion of 55 B.C. Nevertheless, they were never able to fully conquer the people. Subsequent incursions by Caledonians, Anglo-Saxons, Jutes, Danes, Norsemen and Normans have fostered a racial mix of most intrepid adventurers, to the dismay of many foes and subjugated nations around the globe. World wide British possessions and commonwealth nations have included the United States, Canada, portions of South and Central America, India, much of China, Australia, New Zealand, Pakistan, South Africa, Western France, the Rock of Gibraltar, far-flung isles of the sea, Ireland, Israel itself (a notable achievement) and more too numerous to list.

6. The Netherlands

The present day area of the Netherlands was invaded

by Julius Caesar's Romans in the first century B.C. Unable to conquer the elite Batavi and Frisian warriors, Rome made peace with them. Eventually they were accepted into the empire. The Batavi, known for valor, served in the Roman armies as part of the Praetorian Guard. Ethnically distinct from the Belgians and having constantly fortified their borders with Germany, the Dutch, who are one of the smaller nations of Europe have repeatedly distinguished themselves. Their battles for independence, especially under William of Orange in the 1570's mark one of the most outstanding eras in history. Against the greatest of odds, the Dutch brought the notable powers of Europe to the bargaining table on Dutch terms on a number of occasions. Colonial possessions of the Dutch have included New Amsterdam (New York City), New Guinea, portions of South Africa, Surinam and both the East and West Indies.

7. Germany

The Germanic tribes proved to be a bitter pill for the Romans to swallow. After 9 A.D., the Romans were unable to sustain armies there. So fittingly begins the historical saga of a people of warlike souls. Filled with a love of fighting and plunder, the Germans have filled out the ranks of many an ancient and medieval army. But none of the cruel kings and causes they may have served in antiquity had anything on their modern leader, Adolf Hitler and the cruelties of his "third reich". With hundreds of thousands of retarded, senile and handicapped people exterminated, six million Jews slaughtered and over fifty million total dead in World War II, Hitler's Germany eclipsed everything the world had ever seen up to that point in history and set a standard for things to come.

But, in the spirit of the American "GI", Hitler's Wehrmacht millions met their match. Eleven months on the ground from June 6th, 1944 brought an end to Hitler's dreams of world domination. American mass production and a gritty little Jewish or Irish or Polish boy from East Something or other broke the back of Aryan superiority and left a subdued and hollow-eyed silence as the only legacy of Hitler's frenzied lunatic screaming.

8. Austria/Hungary

Subjugated by Tiberius about the year 12 B.C., the Roman province of Pannonia became an immensely important military district until nearly 400 A.D. This same area later became the bedrock of the Austro-Hungarian empire. Founded as the House of Hapsburg in 1278 A.D., the Austro-Hungarian empire was, for several centuries, the richest and most powerful state in Europe. Fragmented since 1918, we look for a continuation of recent changes here (such as Communism's collapse and the Bosnian war.).

9. Russia (Slavic)

Roman incursions into modern day Russia were limited to **the Crimean peninsula and the north shore of the Black Sea** (which was a Roman "lake").

Russia is ethnically Slavic in origin. The Slavs seem to have arisen in the Carpathian mountains, but there has been a tremendous transmigration of the Slavs since the times of antiquity. Today, Slavic people dominate not only Russia, but also Poland, the Ukraine, the Czech Republic, Serbia, Croatia, Byelorussia and a host of other former Soviet republics and their neighbors.

There is a direct Biblical connection to the Russian antiquities and their ancient forbearers. *"Gomer and all his bands..." (Ezekiel 38:6)* is a reference to those tribes living on **the Crimean peninsula and the north shore of the Black Sea**, in what has historically been Russian territory. This is a direct Roman connection. Additionally, Ezekiel's reference to **Meshech** and **Tubal** is a reference to the formerly Soviet cities of Moscow and Tubalsk (Ezekiel 38:2).

The Russian governments have for several hundred years displayed an inordinate interest in the politics of the Holy Land. Going back to the time of the earliest Czars (Russian for Caesar), Russians have felt themselves not only the legitimate successors of the imperial throne, but also the rightful heirs of the authority of the Orthodox Christian faith and therefore protectors of the "holy shrines, icons and relics" in the land of Israel. Yet there has been a simultaneous, recurrent and inexplicable hatred of the Jews throughout Russian history. This has surfaced in pogrom after pogrom and in the policies of support for the enemies of Israel.

Nevertheless, we have cause to be greatly heartened to see the recent progress for the church and for the truth in Russia; especially in the former Soviet Republics. Someone has been praying. God is definitely on the move. We pray that the truth may prosper and that their tranquility may be lengthened.

However, the scriptures are very plain in the proclamation that Gomer, Gog, Meshech and Tubal and all their associated allies are going to come up to battle in the mountains of Israel. Only one sixth part of their army will survive the conflict. May we learn our lessons while there is still time.

10. Antolia (Asia Minor/Turkey)

Several Greek regimes in Asia Minor were overcome by Roman legions in the first or second century B.C. Anatolia (Greek for sun-rising) became known to the Romans as Phrygia and was seat to the eastern empire based in Constantinople. Under attack by the Turks from the tenth century and onward, Constantinople managed to hold out for five hundred more years before finally falling to the Turks in 1453.

Home to the seven churches in Asia noted in Revelation 2, the Anatolian region has been governed by the Turks continuously since 1453. In evidence of their Greco/Roman (like a leopard) heritage, Turkey is today, the only democratic country in all of the Islamic nations. It is also the only Roman horn nation with a Christian heritage in antiquity which is substantially without it (non-Christian) today.

Before we complete our overview of the ten horn nations there are a few concepts we need to emphasize.

The Colonial Powers:

Nearly all of the ten horn nations of Rome have been involved in a not always unified effort at global colonization. Daniel referred to their treading down the whole earth and breaking it in pieces (Daniel 7:23).

In days of antiquity, the Roman emperors organized a thorough treading down of everything that lifted up a heel against them. But it is in modern times that the power of the empire has really come to the forefront. A check of any world map relating to the colonial era will concisely demonstrate the magnitude of the world power these nations have exhibited. For more than four hundred and fifty years they have trampled the whole earth.

There is scarcely a square centimeter of ground in the world and not an island in the sea that has escaped the domination of the European nations. We are not talking about an ancient empire here. This is modern stuff. From Cairo to Cape Town, every flyspeck of African land has been colonially dominated. Prior to the mid-twentieth century, the same was true of Asia. A while previously it was the same in North and South America. It is still true in most of the islands of the sea. Even Antarctica is carved up like a pie chart for America and the nations of Europe.

Certainly there has been a universal trend toward independence being granted to these lands and nations over the past century or so; nevertheless, a lot of Zulu, Inca and Cherokee (etc.) young men went to their graves early in testament to the age of colonialism.

Yet all the wars, tragedies and cruelties of all history are nothing at all to be compared with the things that are in store for this world in the near future. All the nations and kingdoms of this world are swirling around, caught up in the procession of events that are leading up to the inauguration of the "beast" of Revelation, chapter thirteen.

Men are reasonable creatures. God has endued them with reasoning power to think things through and come to logical conclusions. Also He has given us a heart to feel after the emotions that emanate from the soul and enable us to have compassion and love and hope. These and other things that color reason make us what we are when we are at our best.

But **beasts** are not so. The beastly attitude is to seek after pleasure as the uppermost attainment of life. **Beasts** are unreasonable. There is no arguing with a beast. A beast cannot be convinced. They are not governed by compassion.

As many cruel and evil things that the governments of this world have done, yet they were committed by men; men who somewhere had an ounce of human kindness, even if it was only limited to their friends. But all these ten governments of man are soon to give way to a beastly specter not just spiritual - but also embodied in nature. It will be glorious. Degenerate men will glory in the spectacle of this beast. It will be a shining light that the inhabiters of this world will see and worship.

A careful study of the apocalyptic prophesies in the Book of Revelation indicates that upward of three quarters of the world's population will be destroyed during the short reign of this "antichrist" spirit with the nature of a beast. People need to see and understand the nature of this beast before it is too late. The very thought of over four billion people swept away from the earth confounds the mind. Hitler's fifty million pales by comparison. It is time to be sober and serious about living for God.

In all the publicity surrounding the celebration of D-Day's fiftieth anniversary, a good deal of light was shed on the issue of prayer. Americans, French, Canadians, and British alike were aware of the fragility of those first few hours on the beaches of Normandy. There was no question about the justness of the cause. There was no lack of resolve. But the Allied nations were on a course fraught with danger of the first magnitude.

The response, in America at least, was overwhelming.

President Franklin D. Roosevelt came on nationwide radio in that hour with an attitude of prayer. When things were in their most crucial hour, he led the nation to prayer. "Almighty God, (he began) our sons, pride of our nation, this day have set upon a mighty endeavor..." Across the nation, special services were held in nearly every church and cathedral. The pews were full, for the nation had turned their hearts to God for deliverance. God came through for us in that hour.

Franklin Delano Roosevelt

Today we are in no less a period of great national danger. There is an evil tide of wrongfulness of spirit that threatens us. It is striving to destroy our nation, families and friends. More than that, this evil is seeking to destroy our souls. It is time to pray.

It is time for all Americans to wake up spiritually and recognize the danger that is upon us. A thorough understanding of these matters will be absolutely essential in this hour of national dilemma. Let us not let our love of country and things American poison our ability to discern the truth here - or our opportunity to do something meaningful about it.

Thankfulness and Humility.

Chapter V
Another Little Horn

Daniel began to consider the ten horns in the terrible beast. Now we know and have conclusively demonstrated that these ten horns are ten kingdoms (nations) arising out of the Roman empire. We have carefully identified the ten and the time frame of their rise to power. For purposes of clarity we will reiterate that list in condensed form here.

The Ten Horns

Nation	Beginning in Roman Era	Rise to Power
1. Italy	750 B.C.	146 B.C.
2. Spain	200 B.C.	1492 A.D.
3. Portugal	100 B.C.	1445 A.D.
4. France	58 B.C.	638 A.D.
5. Great Britain	55 B.C.	1066 A.D.
6. The Netherlands	58 B.C.	1579 A.D.
7. Germany	1st Century B.C.	843 A.D.
8. Austria/Hungary	12 B.C.	1280 A.D.
9. Russia	100 A.D.	1472 A.D.
10. Anatolia (Turkey)	1st & 2nd Cent B.C.	324 A.D.

In chapter seven, Daniel gives us four separate references to an eleventh horn, the so-called "little horn of Daniel." These references are found in verses 8, 11, 20-21, and 24-25. Each one cross references the other verses and gives additional information. We shall now conclusively demonstrate that the other "little horn" is none other than the United States of America.

In Daniel 7:8 the horn is referred to as "another **little** horn" as it came up among the other ten. This is the only reference we find here as to this horn being little.

When the United States burst upon the international scene in 1776, it was indeed very **little** in the eyes of the rest of the world. The population of the entire U.S. in 1790 was only 3,929,218.[1] At that time and for probably seventy-five years afterward the United States was considered backward and unrefined by the powerhouses of Europe. The U.S. Army was ragtag, composed mostly of part-time soldiers. The only things protecting the fledgling little nation from being annihilated were God Almighty and the expanse of the Atlantic Ocean.

Yet it can fairly be said that the United States came up **among** the other horns per Daniel 7:8. The great preponderance of Americans are ethnically derived from the horn nations of Europe. Since the courts disallowed previous immigration quotas in which European nations were preferred, there has been a wider spectrum of nationalities entering the U.S. but the proportion of Americans with Roman roots is still above eighty percent. So the United States definitely came up from **among** the other ten.

Daniel 7:24 states that the other "king" shall arise **after** the first ten. This is definitely the case with the United States. All ten of the European horn nations had roots back to the Roman era, which the United States obviously does not. The latest blooming of all the other ten (considering when they **arose**) was still 197 years prior to 1776.

This leads us to a greater issue. Daniel 7:24 also states that this eleventh king shall be diverse from the first ten.

---

[1] Statistical Atlas of the United States, (U.S. Government Printing Office, 1914), p. 10.

Right from the very start the United States came into being so very different from what the world had seen before. The old song says:

> My country, 'tis of thee
> Sweet land of liberty
> Of thee I sing
> Land where my fathers died
> Land of the pilgrim's pride
> From every mountainside
> Let freedom ring.

A good percentage of the early founders and European migrators to this country were fleeing religious persecution back home. Two thousand years of hypocrisy and hatred had bred a European power structure that brooked no religious dissent. Martyrs like Joan of Arc, Johann Huss, Michael Servetus, and William Tyndale were burned at the stake for disagreeing with the powers that be. In Catholic Spain and elsewhere they were pulled apart on the rack and various other instruments of torture. Everywhere in Europe the powers that be had learned to distrust all dissent and therefore were ruthless in suppression of it.

Religious movements such as the Quakers, Anabaptists, Puritans, Huguenots, Albigenses, Moravians and in some cases even Catholics were hounded, persecuted and driven from their homelands. There are innumerable stories to tell. By twos and threes, then by the thousands, these humble people fled from oppression. Yet in all Europe there was nowhere they could really go. So when the stories came back of a huge new land of promise, where no kings and no bishops and no inquisitors existed; where the only enemies were elusive savages (natives) and where you could worship God by choice and in freedom - they began to come.

First it was the Puritans to Plymouth Rock in 1620. Then others followed. The Quakers came to Philadelphia, which they termed the city of brotherly love. Yes, America started out different from the first ten nations of Rome.

Another different factor about America was the availability of land. In Europe everything about the land had been sewn up for centuries. The only way to get land was to inherit it. Perhaps by heroic deeds in the wars or by great industry and good luck a person might get some land, but the available quantity was limited and there were many to seek it. Yet in America vacant land was just a stone's throw away from any settlement. Land could be had just for being willing and able to work it. Yes, America was different.

The basic difference was freedom. By this time, Europe was hidebound. It was now fifteen hundred years and better since the Romans had brought "civilization" to the barbaric tribes of Europe. Through all those years men had added laws and rules and customs to life. They endeavored to use the rule of law to cover every eventuality in life and to eliminate all deviations. They just "civilized" themselves out of living room. If you couldn't abide with the status quo in Europe you were in big trouble.

As time progressed the colonies began to be more and more successful in economic matters. At the same time the crowned heads of Europe began to take a larger interest in affairs American. The costs of administration became greater as the colonies grew. The increased population was a tempting target for increased tax revenue. Add to that the fact that all these people were running around unsupervised in America and the result is that nature abhors a vacuum.

Before long there were stamp taxes, poll taxes, tea taxes and fake indians dumping tea into Boston harbor. Everyone knows the result that followed. The American Revolution changed the world.

Showing the Flag:
America's World Domination

Chapter VI
Plucked Up By the Roots

There are three related references in the verses of our study relative to three of the other (original ten) horns.

1. Verse 8: three of the first horns plucked up by the roots before the little horn.
2. Verse 20: refers to three (of the first ten) who fell.
3. Verse 24: notes that *"he shall subdue three kings."*

The **rising** of America **could** be dated to 1776 at the declaration of independence. But generally, in terms of the prophecy here, we don't look at it that way. Many nations (like the Confederacy) have been conceived in an attempted revolution and may have had some reasonable characteristics and bylaws. But all their reasoning is discounted if they cannot survive in the light of day.

This is why we look for not just a birth and an existence, but for a coming to power. Therefore the **rising** of America must date from the first extraterritorial **"pushing"** of the American horn: namely the Spanish-American War. "Remember the Maine" was the battle cry and Teddy Roosevelt's Rough Riders charged up San Juan Hill. The U.S.S. Maine was a new American battleship that blew up and sank in the Havana harbor in 1898 under highly suspicious circumstances. It was never proven whether the Spanish ever blew up the Maine. It could have been an accident.

Theodore "Teddy" Roosevelt of the Bull Moose Party.

In fact, plenty of disinterested parties over the years have concluded that in all probability, it **was** an accident. The Spanish government offered an apology, reparations and really wanted nothing to do with going to war. Nevertheless, the battle cry was "Remember the Maine" and the U.S. would not be mollified. Perhaps there was just a little too much "macho" swaggering around by the Spanish somewhere in the recent past. Whatever, it was off to war.

The American nation had come a long way since the **little** days of the revolution. Of course it was barely noticed abroad when the fledgling nation stood up rather well to the British fleet during the revolution. It was seen more as egg on the British faces. When it happened again in the War of 1812, maybe some people began to wonder. By the time of the Civil War, military experts the world over came to see (and copy) the American ironclads, U.S.S. Monitor and U.S.S. Virginia.

Little wonder then that old Teddy Roosevelt completed his charge successfully. The American navy sent the Spanish fleet to the bottom and suddenly the United States was a world power. In taking possession of Puerto Rico, Guam and the Philippines, the American nation had arisen onto the international scene.

As a result of this war, Spain was totally subdued. Spain has remained very quiet and reserved pertaining to things of the world. Although Adolf Hitler tried very hard to influence them to take his side in World War II, Spain remained neutral in both World Wars.

The Germanic tribes of the old Roman empire days were "hardened to wind and weather in their raw northern climate."[1] They were known for "their native fearlessness and love of war and plunder."[2] For nearly two thousand years they have filled out the ranks of many a conquering army. The Romans, Goths, Franks, Holy Roman Empire, Austro-Hungarians, Prussians and Hohenzollern Kaisers all made use of these fair-headed warlike souls.

In the light of our usage of the term **"arise"**, it could

---

[1] James Breasted and James Robinson, History of Europe, (Boston, Ginn & Co., 1920), p. 290.

[2] Ibid., p. 290.

fairly be said that the German peoples had arisen early in Roman history. Certainly by the reign of Diocletian, Germans had begun to **"push"** in many directions and were thereafter the consternation and dread of much of the Roman world.

Once again by the time of the Hohenzollern kings in the nineteenth century, the Germans were a unified people and were exerting themselves in a most vigorous fashion. They had obtained substantial colonial territories both in Africa and the South Sea Islands of the Pacific Ocean. They had defeated the French in the Franco-Prussian War of 1876. Of course they probably sowed the seeds of their own later defeats by gloating excessively and installing the new emperor in a ceremony at Versailles right after the conquest.

There were a number of militarily strong nations in Europe at the outset of World War I. England, France, Germany, Austria-Hungary, Italy and Russia were all melting down a lot of steel into battleships, cannons and machine guns. Consequently, there was a lot of deviousness and intrigue going on with multi-party treaties and secret alliances. It is no wonder then, that in 1914, push came to shove and the First World War broke out across Europe. Yet when the peace treaties were signed five years later, Germany was blamed for everything.

Under the provisions of the Versailles Treaty, the Germans were forced to give up their naval fleet, surrender all their colonial possessions, allow occupying armies in Germany for years and to pay an enormous amount of war reparations. These reparations were in part responsible for the economic collapse of the German republic some ten years later. Widespread joblessness and hunger followed. Conditions were ripe for Adolf Hitler and his followers.

The history of the Second World War is well known and there is no need for us to dwell on it here. Suffice it to say that **"push"** is a mild term to describe Hitler's Germans in World War II. They were aggressive, vindictive and absolutely ruthless. Whole towns were annihilated, razed and the ground plowed afterwards. Six million Jews were sent to their deaths in the Holocaust. Fifty million people all told perished in the war. Adolf Eichmann (later executed in Israel for his crimes) said he could go laughing into his grave knowing he had been personally responsible for the deaths of two million of those Jewish victims. Untold numbers of Poles, Gypsies, Russians and others were put to death as well. Hitler's followers singled out the mentally insane, retarded, senile, deformed and others they termed useless to society and simply put them to death.

France, Belgium, Holland and Poland collapsed before Hitler's Blitzkrieg in 1939. Britain and Russia barely managed to survive the onslaught but were unable to reverse the tides of Naziism. It was not until the Americans entered the war that Germany was brought to answer for its ways.

The American war machine turned out planes, tanks, guns and ammunition in unprecedented quantities, but it was the American spirit rising up to confront them that the Germans could not withstand. The Americans' strength was in the air as well as on the ground. American planes firebombed cities such as Dresden into ashes. 80,000 people perished in one night! German troops could hardly move anywhere in strength by day because the Americans bombed them out of existence.

Nine months after they landed on the Normandy beaches, the Allies had crushed German resistance. In eleven months, it was over.

Great portions of German territory were permanently ceded to neighboring nations. Germany itself was split into four zones of administration by the conquering powers. Fifty years later, American troops still occupy strategic bases on German soil.

Germany has been totally subdued. Their voice is seldom heard in any question of world politics. Their modestly reconstructed military units stay at home and are remarkably unremarkable. Their infantry in modern times has used donkeys as transport animals. German economic recovery and prosperity has been real, but reserved and low key. They are not flaunting their success.

There is no doubt in any historical sense of the word that it has been the United States that brought about the fall of the German nation and the thorough plucking by the roots of the German spirit. There is no **"push"** left in them and the world knows it.

The Italians came rather late into empire in modern times. In the person of Benito Mussolini they exercised a national longing for the glory days of ancient Rome. The fact that their heart was not into the bloody, down to business side of warmongering did not prevent them from longing for the glory days.

With Mussolini, war was mostly a business of posturing. He would stand up, get loud and bellicose, and make a lot of threats. Western society took him at his word and there was a great fear of him in the twenties and thirties that rivalled the fear of Hitler. Many religionists in western society were having a hard time deciding whether or not Mussolini was actually the antichrist come to head up a revived Roman empire.

The Italians rather showed their weaknesses when they set about to establish a new colonial empire for themselves. Their control in Libya, Ethiopia and Albania grew increasingly difficult for them. When they attempted to invade Greece, the Germans had to come help to save the Italians from a debacle.

By the time the Americans entered the war, Italy had begun the long slide down the losing side of the hill. It took the Americans however, to break the back of Italian military resistance. Russia was busy enough dealing with the Germans and Britain could not sustain an Italian campaign on their own with everything they were already doing. Together, the Americans and British landed in Italy in July 1943 and Italy capitulated shortly thereafter. Mussolini was rescued from capture by the Germans and whisked away to northern Italy to fight on until April of 1945, when he was caught and executed by Italian partisans.

So Italy is the third horn nation that has been subdued by the United States of America. In the fifty years or so since World War II, Italy has shown a long series of short-lived governments. They are not unprosperous, but the **"push"** is gone.

Some have become alarmed over the resurgence of fascist politics in Italy and "skin-head" neo-nazi toughs in Germany. This is a predictable reaction in a society which has had both the moral underpinnings and the national vigorousness cut out from under them. What really ought to concern us is how readily these people will accept the true evil when it comes.

The Great Seal of the United States of America

Chapter VII
The Eyes of Man

We purposefully chose our cover of this book, showing the eye in the pyramid on the Great Seal of the United States.

Daniel spoke of the *"horn that had eyes" (Daniel 7:20)* and that *"in this horn were eyes like the eyes of man." (Daniel 7:8)*.

Now we know that eyes are for seeing. So we are talking about a horn nation with eyes. Not just any eyes, mind you, not beast eyes; but the eyes of a man.

We have already seen in Chapter II concerning the beast which was like a lion (Daniel 7:4), that a man's heart was given to it. We often hear the expression, "have a heart." This is an imploration to show a little human kindness. There has been many a truly "bad" man going about the business of doing evil who was suddenly confronted with a scene of great empathy - causing him to abandon his evil deeds in midstream. He had a heart!

When we consider the beasts of the forest and the jungle which have horns, we recognize that they are somewhat hampered in the use of them. For example, a rhino has very weak vision and relies heavily on the sense of smell. So, although he is very powerful, his power is very limited by his lack of vision.

Rhinoceros
Strong push with weak vision.

Now the little horn has eyes. Not just of a beast, but of a man.

Beasts are reactionary. Basically, they react to whatever they are confronted with. If a man walks up on a watchdog at night, the dog will begin to bark - reacting to the man. If the man leaves, the dog will quiet down and go back to watching. It watches because it is a creature of habit. Either instinctively or as a learned behavior, the dog has a habit of being a watchdog. That is what it will do because it is a beast. As Elvis Presley used to sing, "You ain't nothin' but a hound dog." Don't expect anything more out of it.

But a man is created in a different way by the Lord: He **is** capable of reacting and being a creature of habit. But a man is more than that: He was created just a little lower than the angels. A man can see. He can see more than what is just on the surface. A man can see past the immediate to recognize the resultant. This is why prophets in ancient times were called **seers**. They could see. It is a reasoned response but it is also a seeing response.

For example, Archimedes wrestled with a problem of how to detect whether supposedly pure gold had been fraudulently alloyed with silver or copper. He couldn't find the answer until one day he was taking a bath. Suddenly he "saw" the answer. All he saw was his body dipped in the water. But suddenly he **"saw"** the relationship between volume (that could be measured by displaced water) and weight. He cried out, "Eureka!" (I have found it!).

So the little horn has the eyes of a man. The little horn can see a situation and not just react.

In the American case, a good example would be in the treatment of vanquished foes. In World War II, the United States and Russia bore down on Nazi Germany from opposite points of the compass. Germany was utterly defeated and at the mercy of the victors. There is no doubt that the Germans were guilty of absolutely horrid and inhuman crimes. Punishment was the order of the day and the Russians set about it in a very thorough way. They shot great numbers of Germans on sight, looted the entire countryside of everything that could be carted off and were cruel masters indeed.

On the other hand, the Americans could "see" that there was a better policy. The Americans saw past the immediate circumstances to somehow recognize the resultant. While in no way lenient toward the actual perpetrators of German atrocities, the United States did not let the blame unduly pass over to the general population. Starving German civilians were allowed to eat U.S. Army rations at many Army mess halls. The destitute were clothed and given temporary housing. The immediate result was droves of Germans flocking to surrender to the Americans and fleeing the Russians. The long term result was the ascendancy of American policies rather than Russian ones.

So the American nation has eyes in its horn. When the Americans get to **"pushing,"** they can **"see"** what they are doing. They don't just use blind force and go around goring and trampling other countries in a reactionary rage. It makes a big difference.

Concerning the great American seal; people who are spiritual in nature - and not everyone is - know that sign and substance frequently have a connection to things of the future. Wordsworth said, "The child is father of the man." Events which happen when we are young shape our character when we are old. We need to learn to read the sign posts along the way.

What this means in plain English is that, much like diplomatic sign language, there are signs of a spiritual nature which, if we are aware of them, will give us insight into things to come. This may not always be good. Some let this degenerate into watching for black cats and broken mirrors and letting such things affect their lifestyle. But there is a better way.

Did the designers and the engraver of the Great Seal of the United States have foresight when they put this thing together? Was there guidance from, say, the watchers in heaven (Daniel 4:23)? What motivated them? Several changes were made during the process. We don't want to speculate here. For the present we notice:

1. A structure (pyramid) that could be said to bear resemblance to a horn and which appears to be little.

2. In it the eye of a man.

3. A Latin inscription, signifying first, a heritage of the Roman empire, and also, a new world order.

4. For the present we can go no farther.

Thomas Jefferson, Third American President: Writer of the Declaration of Independence.

Chapter VIII
A Mouth Speaking Great Things

A thousand nations must have been born at one time or another throughout history. They have come and gone. But unless you count the five books of Moses, there has never been a nation that was inaugurated with words like those accompanying the birth of the American nation.

"We hold these truths to be self-evident: That all men are created equal: that they are endowed, by their creator, with certain inalienable rights; that among these are life, liberty and the pursuit of happiness...

That... governments (derive) their just powers from the consent of the governed."

These are profound concepts. True concepts. The world stood up and took notice. Nothing like this had ever been heard from existing governments, let alone new ones.

"All men are created equal."
The pauper is as good a man as the king. The cripple is as good a man as the athlete. This is a spirit observation. The natural eye and the natural mind would reject such a thought. But it is a spiritual truth. This is why a crippled man like Franklin D. Roosevelt can be a great president. This is why Steven Hawking can be an eminent scientist. In a spiritual way all men are created equal. No one is limited by their circumstances. Amazing!

"Governments (derive) their just powers from the consent of the governed."
This too, is an amazing principle. At the time most European kings believed they ruled by "divine right". In other words, God gave them the **right** to be king. The common people had nothing to do with it. Their purposes and consent were immaterial. Another school thought it was by reason, you had to convince people by sound logic in order to govern them. This is an unfortunate idea. We need to be obedient whether we understand or not. But government by the consent of the governed? Unheard of.

Actually this (also profound) way **is the way God set up.** God Himself does not force us to do things His way. If He wanted robots He would have made them. He wants people who will make the right choices. But He does not force them on us. Remember when Jesus Himself could not do mighty works in His hometown? He marvelled because of their unbelief (Mark 6:5-6).

If people don't believe in the government and consent to it, it is incapable of governing. If no one will call the police, they can not keep the peace and enforce the law. If no one will call the fire department, the house will burn down. If leading citizens of the city will not communicate with the mayor and the council, how will the city be governed? The answer is: incorrectly, inadequately and inefficiently.

"No title of nobility shall be granted by the United States."

In the kingdoms of Europe there was and is a titled nobility: Duke and duchess, counts and countesses, kings and queens. Some of these positions were hereditary, passed down to the next generation. Some were positions of favor with the king or some honor from him. All these people were considered to be better than the common people - a cut above the rest.

This created a tangled mess. Privileged people expected and got special treatment. In his auto-biography, Benjamin Franklin cited a governor of the colonies prior to the revolution whose authority was required in order to pass any tax levy to fund the government. Yet he would only consent if a special provision of the tax law exempted he and his peers from the tax.[1]

---

[1] The Autobiography of Benjamin Franklin, (New York, Prestige Books,

The U.S. Constitution prohibited the establishment of such a nobility (Article I sec. 9). No one was to have privilege above anyone else. Everyone is supposed to be equal before the law.

Perhaps of all the great things ever uttered as the law and official pronouncements of the United States Government, nothing has been more sweeping in its application than the Bill of Rights: the first ten amendments to the Constitution.

Even the concept of human "rights" themselves had never been articulated in this way before. The English Magna Charta (1215 A.D.) had established principles relative to the liberty of the individual. The Roman law of the Twelve Tables (450 B.C.) was established to correct injustices affecting the common man. But these earlier compilations; while they addressed grievances, they did so by law. The law was pre-eminent. The administration (and administrator) of the law was the seat of authority.

In this concept of "rights", the United States proclaimed to the world the existence of a higher moral authority than the law. This was not an appeal to Sovereign God, other than to recognize God as the Creator of these things; but it was very far reaching indeed.

We need to emphasize here that there is a great difference between the spirit and the physical reality. We are beginning to deal here with the "spirit of America" on one level and the physical reality of the American Nation on another.

1968), p. 203.

Everyone who lives in America deals with a microcosm of the physical reality every day. Our neighbor, friend, spouse and children are all part of the physical reality. But we also deal with elements of the spirit of America every day as well. This is more likely to come across in cultural ways such as sports, music, journalism, politics etc.

In one sense we are very familiar with our families. We know all about the corner grocery store, Main Street, Yellowstone Park, Disney World and the space shuttle. This is the physical America we rub shoulders with every day. But there is another sense of America that touches all these things and we need to establish the reality of it. That sense is the "spirit" of America.

Declaring the Spirit of America.

Chapter IX
The Spirit of America

One of the greatest concepts of Bible Study is cross referencing. One of the principal precepts is;

"In the mouth of two or three witnesses shall every word be established." (II Corinthians 13:1).

Moses, Christ and Paul all noted this great principle. In Daniel, chapter seven, the great words of the little horn are cross referenced for us (four times in one chapter):

Verse 8: *"a mouth speaking great things."*
Verse 11: *"the great words which the horn spake."*
Verse 20: *"a mouth that spake very great things."*
Verse 25: *"and he shall speak great words against the most high."*

It would have been very wonderful and noble indeed if the official voices of the United States of America had spoken about "all men created equal," and "inalienable rights," and "fourscore and seven years ago," and stopped there. But there is a progression involved. You can see the signs of this progression in just about everything American. Let's look at a couple of examples.

Seventy years ago, more or less, the motion pictures were showing Keystone Cops and Tom Mix. Most people thought it was great. But they didn't stop there. They went on to the Little Rascals and then to "Gone with the Wind," with cursing on the screen. Before too many years it was not just an occasional curse, it was "Who's Afraid of Virginia Wolf?" filled with wild tirades of cursing. There's been a corresponding escalation of violence. Things have gone from cowboys punching and shooting each other to "Psycho," then to the "Texas Chain Saw Massacre" and worse and worse. There is a compelling drive to more violence, more sex, more corruption and all the better if they're all in the same movie. Progressively the American people want to see more and more of it.

Another example would be television. Years ago it was "Leave It to Beaver" and "Father Knows Best" (in which they were pointing out that he didn't). The progression was to Andy Griffith. Everyone likes a good laugh. But now the humor has become more violent, dirtier and has lost its moral linchpins. Television soap operas have grown seamier and steamier. Talk show hosts see who can break the most taboos and expose the most lurid sex scandals for the whole country to view. It is a progression; a downward spiral before our eyes.

Let's go back and look at the Declaration of Independence and the framers of the constitution for a moment. The founding fathers went through a rather protracted series of meetings in working out the language of these famous documents. Before every meeting they prayed. This was their custom both before and after independence. Whenever there was an important meeting, they always opened with prayer.

How then, and with what logic did the Supreme Court decide that these men, who opened every meeting with prayer and mentioned God several times in the major documents, ever intended the constitution to prohibit prayer in the public schools or in the government? It is inconceivable that the men who opened every meeting drafting the constitution with prayer should be intending to ban it thereafter.

Nevertheless there are some stories which have not been front page, but are still true. There is no doubt that the framers of the constitution were not all of one mind. Thomas Jefferson was a noted exception.

Jefferson had his own particular set of religious beliefs. He believed that there was a God and that He should be worshipped. But he believed it ought to be done in private only. Jefferson believed the Bible, at least certain parts of it. Then he decided that the Bible needed to have a new version; an edited version. So he set about to make one himself. We don't want to be critical. So let's just recognize that there is a progression here.

America as an entity didn't start out life speaking great words against the Most High any more than movies started out pornographic or television started out vulgar. Paul told Timothy that *"in the last days, perilous times would come, evil men and seducers would wax worse and worse." (II Timothy 3:13)*.

There is only one instance in the Bible where anyone was forbidden to pray by law and that is in the case of Daniel (in the lion's den). So we must suppose, if Daniel's case had come up before the Supreme Court, they would have upheld the verdict of the lower court and also cast Daniel into the lion's den.

The Supreme Court's decision involved great words. We know they were great words because of all the stir and commotion they caused. The nation still has not forgotten all these years later. Someone might say that the court didn't ban prayer, it just banned organized prayer. By this standard, Franklin D. Roosevelt's D-Day prayer on nationwide radio was unconstitutional and illegal.

This is how the nation began speaking great words against the Most High.

Let's take another example; the "women's liberation" movement. Radical feminism is definitely in the category of great words against the Most High. Nature is something we ought to take into consideration. Nature is the way God made things. If God ever wants to supersede nature, like in our sexual mores, He goes to a lot of trouble to say so.

Nature tells us that men ought to take the leading role. Man is on average, bigger than the woman. He weighs more than the woman. He is stronger physically, runs faster, jumps higher and quite a few more things. All this is nature at work. Even in young children, the boys seem to be more forceful and aggressive. It is no wonder then, that in six thousand years of recorded history, men have gravitated to the leading role.

There is a reason why the first forty-two presidents have all been men. Looking back at history, there is a reason why the tremendous preponderance of statesmen, monarchs, inventors, scientists, mathematicians, rich people, beggars and thieves have been men. The reason is nature; human nature. God created the man to lead and the woman to help.

Chauvinism, according to Webster, is a term taken from the life of Nicholas Chauvin of Rochefort, France, a soldier in the First Republic and Empire. This man's demonstrative patriotism and attachment to Napoleon came to be ridiculed by his comrades.

We take it then, that a male chauvinist in the strict sense of the word, would be some ridiculous person who has an overly demonstrative faith and attachment in the ascendancy of men.

This is an extremely distorted view. History is not made of groups of men-lovers trying to exclude women. Men spend their better years trying to love women. Nature's way is for a man to fall in love with a woman. When a man loves a woman he becomes one of nature's most amazing creatures - a suitor.

> *"There be three things which are too wonderful for me, yea four which I know not: The way of an eagle in the air; the way of a serpent upon a rock; the way of a ship in the midst of the sea; and the way of a man with a maid." (Proverbs 30:18-19)*

Nature works in such a way that it is the woman who physically bears the children. This ties up nine months of her life in a very real way. It is the woman who nurtures and feeds the baby. It's the mother's instinct to hover around and love her child and tend to all the needs of the child. It is natural for the wife to love her husband, yet the scriptures go past love and command the wives to be in subjection to their husbands (Ephesians 5:22). We cannot argue with the scriptures.

What we find in "women's liberation" is substantial numbers of women who want to reject the natural way and the scriptural way. They reject the Bible, reject "Adam's rib", reject the words of the Savior and the words of the Holy Spirit through the pen of Saint Paul. They even reject nature itself. When things progress this far, they have come a long way (baby), but the direction is steeply down.

There have been something over twenty-five million abortions in the United States since the Supreme Court decision on "Roe v. Wade" in 1973. That amounts to twenty-five million young people who would have been in existence today but are not. That is seventeen times more people than the country has lost in all wars put together. It is eight times more people than have **ever** died in traffic accidents in America.

Many women who have had an abortion say that while they made a rational decision to have the "procedure" done, they were not at all prepared for the surprising depth of the emotional trauma involved.

Of course, this is due to the fact that they are taking a life. True, that life is entrusted to their care so long as they are carrying the child. But there is a deeper issue than what meets the eye here. The birth of a child is much more than the spontaneous result of a man and a woman coming together.

First, we must realize that the spirits come out from God before they ever get to the mother's womb. God told Jeremiah, *"before I formed thee in the belly I knew thee," (Jeremiah 1:5)*. Also we know that God is the Father of spirits (Hebrews 12:9) and that the spirits return to God who gave them when life is over (Ecclesiastes 12:7).

Second, we must recognize that there is a conception process. The woman has to conceive a child before the child can exist. This is a hard concept until we think of it as just that - a concept. The concept of long division has to be mastered in the mind before the problems can be worked out with a pencil. By the same token, a child is more than biological chemistry. The child has to be conceived in a woman - spirit, mind and body, before becoming a reality.

Now, science is giving us test tube babies, where the chemistry part is taking place in a lab somewhere. But a real life mother still has to bring that child into the world from the womb. She still has to conceive, no matter what the test tube says.

Of course, people were already having abortions prior to Roe v. Wade. Mainly it was either done illegally or in Sweden (or other countries where it was legal). Then seven men in the Supreme Court bypassed the normal aspects of lawmaking and introduced this horrid practice to an unsuspecting society. Now abortions are being performed all over the world. This is wickedness.

The natural process of debate never took place prior

to the Supreme Court foisting this nightmare onto society. One of the safeguards in the legislative system is the debate. When the courts start legislating, they are trespassing. It ought not to be. They are not constitutionally qualified to pass sweeping new legislation by edict.

The issue of whether or not to have abortions in this nation ought not to be entrusted to seven votes in the Supreme Court. It ought not be the decision of mentally distraught young women who failed to weigh all the factors beforehand and fell into sin. Two wrongs don't make a right. It certainly ought not to be decided in the news media. In fact, it never should have been decided in the first place. It ought to have been left alone.

Ronald Reagan, one of the brightest stars ever to grace American politics, wrote an excellent book on this whole issue, **Abortion and the Conscience of the Nation,** Thomas Nelson, Publisher, 1984). It should be required reading in every classroom in America.

One of the greatest problems with abortion is that it is a bottomless pit issue. The unborn child is human. That is a human life! It doesn't matter if the child is crippled, has Down's syndrome, is unwanted or whatever else. Once a decision is made to take a life, we have opened the bottomless pit.

Among the twenty-five million plus unborn children who have already perished may have been the one who was going to find a cure for cancer. Maybe one was a statesman who would have saved the nation from destruction. Whenever we destroy life we are destroying possibilities.

So at what point is it o.k. to take this human life? Is it 180 days, or 150, 120, 90 days? The Supreme Court made a decision as to when the life of the child could be self-sustaining. But there are unscrupulous doctors right now, who for money will do third trimester abortions (The love of money is the root of all evil.). If there wasn't big money in it, you could hardly find a doctor to do abortions.

Ronald Reagan's book, which also featured pieces by C. Everett Koop and Malcolm Muggeridge, predicted that opening the abortion issue would eventually lead to opening the euthanasia issue. Less than ten years later it has already been proven true. When that door was opened, it was not even limited to those who were terminally ill. Right away they started "assisting" the suicides of people with multiple sclerosis and other such problems which are debilitating but not necessarily fatal. It is very disturbing to see videos of people walking around, talking, possessed of all their faculties - then laying down to breathe in the deadly vapors of carbon monoxide.

The next step (and it is only a step away) is moving on to people who cannot be classified as suicidal. Adolf Hitler emptied the insane asylums and nursing homes in his drive to eliminate sub-human elements and worthless lives. May God spare us and the nation!

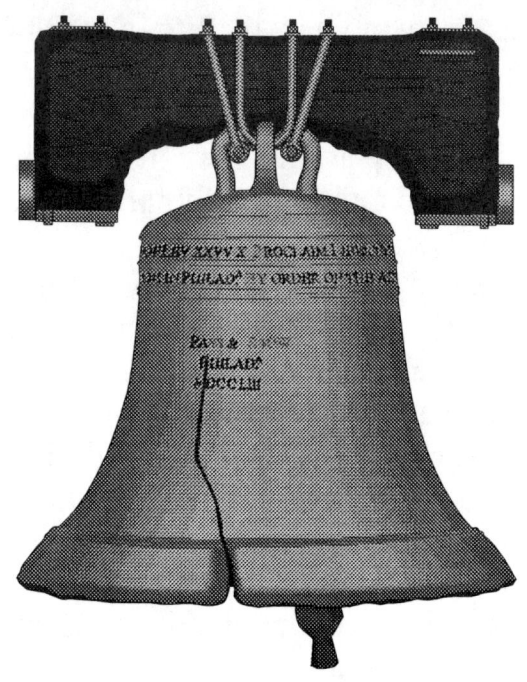

The Liberty Bell

Chapter X
Jesus Is Coming

The Second Coming of our Lord and Savior, Jesus Christ, is our pre-eminent hope in this world. We cannot trust in material things. We can't take them with us when we die. We can't give ourselves over to pleasures, for they are fleeting. We can't put out hope in any other person in this world. They too are mortal and will soon be gone. We certainly can't afford to trust in ourselves. So, let our glory be in the cross and let our hope be in His coming.

There is nothing concerning the kingdoms of this world that we can cling to. The institutions of government are feeble and incapable of generating our salvation.

The United States brought forth liberty on this continent in 1776. But when the famous and specially cast "Liberty Bell" was rung, it cracked. This flawed earthly liberty cannot carry us into the heavenlies. We have to step up to a higher level and let Jesus Christ be our salvation.

There has been a lot of talk about the rapture in religious circles over the years and increasingly so now, given the signs of the times. More serious heed ought to be given to the scriptures so that we can follow the words of Christ on this subject. We might say that the word, "rapture," does not appear in the scriptures anywhere. It is a coined phrase someone invented to identify the return to earth which Jesus Himself predicted.

In Luke 17:26-36, we find a definitive description of the process in the Savior's own words. He starts by comparing His return to earth to the days of Noah. Noah preached the flood for a hundred years before it happened. People were too busy eating, drinking, marrying and giving in marriage. We see the same conditions today. Eating and drinking and multiple marriages are the norm. Even gas stations have turned into food emporiums. It should be noted here that we have been preaching the Second Coming of the Savior for over ninety years now.

Some years ago, there was a tremendous natural disaster when Mt. St. Helens erupted in Washington State. With a blast five hundred times greater than a nuclear bomb, an entire cubic mile of solid rock mountain was vaporized in a moment of time. Yet the headlines in many papers that day read, "RIOTS IN MIAMI!" It's easy to let ourselves get distracted by false commotions into missing the real thing when it happens.

Jesus likened His Coming to the days of Lot.

> *"But the same day that Lot went out of Sodom it rained fire and brimstone from heaven, and destroyed them all. Even thus shall it be in the day when the Son of man is revealed. In that day, he which shall be upon the housetop and his stuff in the house, let him not come down to take it away; and he that is in the field, let him likewise not return back. Remember Lot's wife." (Luke 17:29-32)*

There is a common misconception concerning the rapture that came from men's minds and not from the scriptures. Many people believe they'll just be riding along in their car and suddenly, "Poof! Twinkle!" the rapture will happen. Cars will wreck all over the highways because drivers have disappeared. Graves will rip open and coffin lids fly everywhere and we'll all be gone. But this is careless theology.

When Jesus resurrected, there was an earthquake and an angel rolled the stone away. That was for the benefit of the disciples. They needed the stone rolled back so they could see. Stones were no barrier to the Lord, who later entered a locked room with the door barred in the presence of His disciples. When the saints put on a glorified body, we will be like Him. We will take on His attributes and share in His glory. Paul definitely said that this event will take place in a moment and the twinkling of an eye (I Corinthians 15:52). We also have to keep things focused and in context.

We also know that Jesus stated clearly that **no** man knows the day or the hour of his Coming, no not the angels in heaven. The Father has reserved this knowledge unto Himself. (Consequently **anyone** who sets a date is wrong - disregard them.)

Nevertheless the Spirit of God is doing a great work in these last days. There is no doubt some who are living close enough to the Savior that they are going to have advance intimate knowledge of His imminent return without knowing the day or the hour. The Holy Spirit is dealing this closely and on this level with men right now and in ways that were not known just a short time ago. That is not to say the day is imminent (as a snare it will come) but the pace of the race is accelerating exponentially.

A word of caution: if you are dealing with spirits, you'd better be mighty sure of which ones you are dealing with. I John 4:1 warns:

"Beloved, believe not every spirit, but try the spirits whether they are of God: because many false prophets are gone out into the world."

The Apostle Paul, no doubt the most spiritually gifted example we have, was struck down and in great light confronted by the Savior on the road to Damascus. Note his response. *"Who art thou, Lord?"* And note the reply. *"I am Jesus whom thou persecutest."*

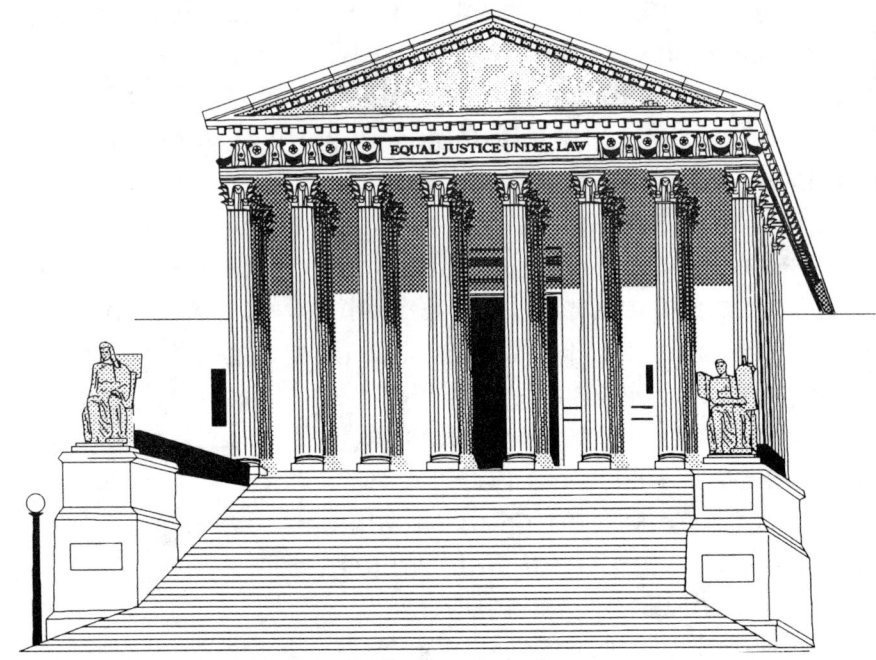

The U. S. Supreme Court

Chapter XI
Made War with the Saints

"I beheld, and the same horn made war with the saints, and prevailed against them;" (Daniel 7:21)

There is a great difference between making war with the **saints** and making war with the **church**.

Jesus entered into a discussion with His disciples (Matthew 16:13-18) in which He asked them, *"Whom do men say that I the Son of man am?"* Because of the miracles He was performing and the effect on their consciousness, men were of the opinion that somehow Jesus was not only Himself, but also was the reincarnation of some great figure of the past. Some thought He was John the Baptist (never mind that they lived concurrently for over thirty years and that John baptized Jesus). Some thought He was Elijah come back to earth. Others thought He was Jeremiah or one of the other old prophets.

Then Jesus asked the pre-eminent question of His ministry. Knowledge of the answer to this question is the doorway to all greater spiritual insight, power and destiny. *"But whom say ye that I am?" (Matthew 16:15)*. Simon Peter did not hesitate. He spoke right up.

> *"Thou art the Christ, the son of the living God. And Jesus answered and said unto him, Blessed art thou, Simon BarJona: for flesh and blood hath not revealed it unto thee, but my Father which is in heaven. And I say also unto thee, that thou art Peter, and upon this rock I will build my church: and the gates of hell shall not prevail against it." (Matthew 16:13-16).*

As we said before, there is a great difference between making war against the **saints** and making war against the **church**. Jesus said the gates of hell shall not prevail against the church. But speaking through Daniel, the Lord said that the little horn *"made war against the saints and prevailed against them."*

When one is born again of the water and the Spirit they become a saint of the Most High. When two or three or more saints get together and fellowship or go to the store together, they are having a social event. But when those same two or three are gathered together in the Name of the Lord, then He is in the midst of them

(Matthew 18:20). At that point they begin having "church."

The devil had probably already sized up Adam in the Garden of Eden and decided he couldn't get him to eat the fruit first, so he went after Eve. When God wouldn't allow Satan to attack Job's person, he went after his children and his possessions. Likewise, being unable to prevail against the church, Satan has targeted the individual saints.

Now the church consists of more than just the individual saint. If the saint **was** the church, Jesus would have said when **one** is gathered in My Name, there will I be in the midst. But the church begins to function when two or more are gathered in His Name. The Spirit begins to move in and around them.

The main function and purpose of the church is to give glory and honor unto the King (Jesus is King of kings and Lord of lords.) and to facilitate salvation among mankind. In fact, these are the reasons for all of creation. But a substantial portion of the creation has refused to glorify God, namely the devils and the sinners among men. Therefore, God has ordained that His church would show forth the praises of the King.

> *"And to make all men see what is the fellowship of the mystery, which from the beginning of the world hath been hid in God, who created all things by Jesus Christ: to the intent that now unto the principalities and powers in heavenly places might be known by the church the manifold wisdom of God." (Ephesians 3:9-10)*

There is a fellowship that takes place as the church

service is in progress. The saints are involved in a fellowship in the Spirit. This is a joint fellowship of all the saints worshipping together. In this fashion they become the Body and Bride of Christ.

Just as it takes all the blocks in the walls fitting together to make up a building, so is the church. Just as it takes all the cells in the human body to make up the body, so is the church. All the cells interact through the blood. All the cells have something to add to the body and the body adds the ministration of life through the blood to every cell. We are more than stones, we are lively stones.

> *"Ye also, as lively stones, are built up a spiritual house, an holy priesthood, to offer up spiritual sacrifices, acceptable unto God by Jesus Christ." (I Peter 2:5)*

That priesthood, the spiritual sacrifices and the reality of **church** all begin to take place as that interaction starts flowing between the saints. It is just as real and vital with two as it is with two thousand (abortion at any stage is a grievous sin). When the precious blood of Christ flows between the saints it sparks and livens the whole body.

When Jesus told Peter, *"upon this rock I will build my church,"* He was referring to more than just Peter. In the Greek, the name, Peter, means "little rock." But Jesus was speaking Aramaic. The essential part of the church was not Peter, it was the blood. The life is in the blood (Genesis 9:4).

When Peter said, *"thou art the Christ,"* he was doing his part to open the avenue for the blood. Jesus said, *"thou art Peter."* When an individual saint establishes a one-on-one relationship with Jesus (I know you and you know me) they are born again. It is a process involving faith, repentance, water baptism and Holy Spirit infilling.

When two or more saints get together and begin to interact with the Spirit and the blood, they begin to have church. There is life in the blood. There is power in the blood!

Now it is written that the gates of hell shall not prevail against the church (whole body). But it is also written (we reiterate) that the little horn prevailed against the **saints**. The method of attack is to wear them out; *"and shall wear out the saints of the Most High." (Daniel 7:25)*.

A healthy body can withstand just about anything. The body has natural defenses which enable it to do so. Whether it might be heat, cold, rain, snow, injury, disease or sickness; the body has defenses to ward them off. If an exterior enemy or wild animal comes against the body, there are defenses that can be activated.

But when fatigue sets in, the defenses can be overwhelmed. When someone becomes "worn-out" either from temporary or long-term overexertion or from old age, then they are susceptible to all kinds of attack.

Make no mistake about the origins of these attacks. Attacks against the saints originate from Satan. But from the earliest times, Satan has used an agent. Coming against Eve, he used the subtility of the serpent to disguise his attack. Against Job, he utilized the Chaldeans and a great wind, among other things. Usually Satan disguises his attacks in surrogate-ly deceptive ways. Once, however, in the temptation of the Lord Jesus, Satan came in person.

Satan tempted Jesus by offering to give Him the power and glory of all the kingdoms of the world. For he said, *"to whomsoever I will I give it."* *(Luke 4:1).*

Now Jesus did not succumb to the devil's temptations. But in tempting the Lord, Satan showed his hand by offering a prize worthy of the occasion. Through this we recognize that the kingdoms of this world are not organized by chance; but Satan is at work in them. It is the devil that has caused so much shame and degradation among the nations.

When Hitler organized the methodical mass-murder of six million Jews, we know it was the work of the devil. When the Spanish Inquisition tortured untold thousands we know that the devil was behind it. These obvious cases stick out like sore thumbs. But the devil does not always come murdering and torturing. The devil does his dirtiest work in a tuxedo.

If Satan can get great masses of people condemned to hell simply by deception and enticements, he will do it. Historically, the main times he resorts to mayhem is when the other methods aren't working, or when his murderous nature sticks out. He was a murderer from the beginning (John 8:4).

This is why much of the devilment in America today takes on such a coat and tails aura. The great majority of the American nation is going to hell in a hay wagon. There is an unprecedented level of hate, murder, adultery, fornication, uncleanness, homosexuality, theft, abortion, and just plain lusting sinfulness going on at all levels of society. There has been a tremendous rise in mediums dealing with familiar spirits. The saints of the Most High are being worn out by the incessant attacks.

We are going to have to examine the mechanism

behind this assault. How is the U.S.A. in spirit, making war with the saints? How are we being worn out, being prevailed against?

One only has to examine the treatment given to the native American Indians to recognize that everything about America is not all sweetness and light. When the pilgrims and others first arrived on these shores, they found the native peoples to be friendly and helpful. Whether it was Squanto and Samoset saving the Pilgrims or Pocahontas saving Captain John Smith, early relations with the Indians were not unfriendly. Rather, Indians reacted to brutal treatment from the whites. A number of excellent histories can be studied to fill out the story of the American Indian and how he was treated, cheated and left on the ashdump of history by a greedy nation.

If we go on briefly to remember the history of the treatment America gave to the black Africans; through slavery and prejudice for over two centuries, we will realize that there is an undercurrent of wrongfulness woven into the American spirit. Denial and whitewashing the fact will not change the truth. Noble ideals are no substitute for down to earth results. All the rhetoric and government plums of the past few years have not eliminated the basic facts. There are still a lot of problems. The majority of blacks in this country still are not doing all that well. Food stamps and welfare are no substitute for equal opportunity.

War Against Expression of Faith

When we begin to consider the case of the warring attacks of the American little horn, we must remember the saints are not being crushed. We are being worn out. There is no Colosseum full of lions, no horrid physical menace destroying our lives. There is just a real daily pressure that grinds our gears until we are unable to go anymore. We get worn out.

There is a great need in the heart of every saint of God to praise the Lord. It just needs to come welling up from down in the soul and bring release and realization of the goodness of Jesus.

This is why the American Supreme Court's anti-prayer decision of **war against expression of faith** is such a detrimental grind to the saints of God. Yet it is only symptomatic of the greater pressures of society and the social spirit.

No amount of logic can explain why the Supreme Court banned prayer in the public schools. The first amendment protects freedom of speech. Evidently religious speech, or specifically prayer is not to be free. It is exempted. You can pray anywhere, but not at school. You can lead prayers anywhere, but not at school. A person would think that, given the current conditions in the nation's schools, they could use a little prayer.

Atheists have been allowed to come to school and give anti-God harangues. The students **have** to listen to that garbage. The person who initiated the lawsuit against public school prayer is a noted atheist who has been allowed to speak in numerous schools.

Witches have been allowed to speak at public schools. Homosexuals are allowed and in some cases, encouraged to come to school and teach their evil ways. It seems that any morality at all is fine for the public schools as long as it isn't Christian morality.

The decision against school prayer is a landmark. It is symbolic of a much larger anti-God bias in society. By coming out against prayer, the court was also by inference weighing in against all things Godly in nature. They backed this up later by banning manger scenes (creches) at Christmas time in all government buildings and on the grounds thereof.

The Supreme Court is in a position of leadership in American government. When they take a stand on an issue, it has repercussions throughout society. Supposedly they consider this in the back rooms where they hash out these decisions among "themselves." But when such a notable part of government speaks, the nation responds.

This is a spirit which has caught on in America. It's a spirit that says, "I don't care if **you're** religious, but leave **me** out of it." It's a spirit that puts a "no soliciting" sign on the front door. It's a spirit that is open to every wind of change but goes to great lengths to **ward off the truth**. It's amazing to think that anyone, let alone a whole nation would want to ward off the truth; but it's happening in America today.

America has put up the no soliciting signs, fences in the front yards, pit bulls and security systems to ward off the truth. Affluent sub-communities have gate guards and electronics, while even the poorest communities are going to elaborate fencing to close themselves off. Some say no, it's to ward off burglars, thieves and crooks. But thievery is still thriving.

An affluent golf and residential community in North Carolina was recently shocked to discover that someone had driven up to the front security gate, shot and killed the guard, then drove on in to one of the residences, broke in and murdered one of the residents in cold blood. There is no defense against behavior like this.

The simple truth is: it doesn't matter what defense

mechanisms we install. Even the president with armored limousines and heavy secret service protection is not secure. There have been at least four attempts on the lives of the last eight presidents. One succeeded (John Kennedy) and one nearly did (Ronald Reagan). Afterwards Reagan said he had come to realize that if someone out there was willing to trade his life for yours, there was not a lot you could do about it.

As an extension of this logic, you are not safe in your car either. Drive-by random shootings, car-jackings and the like have exposed this fact. A lot of these crazed killers care nothing for your life. If you don't get out of your car when they wave a pistol, they will fill you full of lead and never shed a tear. The fact that they are not acting alone; that there is a spirit behind their actions is proof to us and inconsequential to them.

In foreign countries some of the more vulnerable government and industry leaders have taken to riding around in armored caravans when they go to work. This too is no sure defense. Assailants have taken to obliterating entire caravans with massive explosive-laden car bombs along the route and to attacking vehicles with armor-piercing machine guns and rocket launchers. It is coming here; on the way.

You are not safe on the job. Disgruntled employees who have been fired are proving this ever so succinctly. A recent post office rampage by a disgruntled fired worker in Royal Oak, Michigan left many of his co-workers dead and wounded. Yes, he killed at least two of the supervisors he hated, but also killed and wounded a number of innocent bystanders.

You're not safe in a restaurant. In a symptomatic case recently in Fayetteville, North Carolina, a drunken G.I.

from Ft. Bragg came into a restaurant brandishing an armload of guns and began shooting. Before he was shot and wounded himself (not seriously), he had killed the owners of the restaurant and several customers while wounding several more.

All these incidents might seem to be random and insane but that is not the case. There is a spirit at work in America today and it is not a friendly spirit.

The reason people want to ward off the truth in America is because they can't stand it. The truth cuts across the grain of the way most American people are living and they can't stand to confront it. This is the real reason people don't want us coming to their door. This is why phone numbers are unlisted. This is why the pit bulls and cordoned communities are there.

Time was in America, and not that long ago, when people were open and honest hearted. If we came up to someone's house on a summer's evening, we'd likely find them out on their front porch, maybe doing a pleasant little chore and just being neighborly. Time was, and not all that long ago, that we knew all the neighbors and took time to be friendly and considerate. Today, if we come up to a neighbor's house, they are probably inside watching some devilment on T.V.

Truth

Why are Americans so intent on warding off the truth? As we said, it is because they can't stand it. The truth is, adultery and fornication are wrongful sins, violate nature's trust and are carrying Americans to hell. But people don't want to hear it. The truth is, homosexuality is a crime against nature. It is the cause of the spread of the AIDS epidemic. Truth is, if they would just completely cease from illicit sex, the spread of AIDS would be completely halted. The truth is, American people would do better to turn off their televisions and start spending those six hours a day in prayer and other useful things. But they don't want to hear it. They would rather have illiterate children, a house full of other people's sins to watch and partake of and no time to do the things that could make a difference in life.

Truth is, American people ought to be in church and seeking the face of the Lord. Preachers ought to get off the "fence" and label sin for what it is. They ought to quit sugar coating the gospel, put the Word of God on the line and demand that the people live up to it.

Truth is, there is an American spirit at work warding off the truth so that people can go about their business of being evil. We can call it political correctness, the social gospel, new ageism, coolness or popularity. What ever it is called, Americans need to quit warding off the truth, get down on their knees before God and repent and pray that God will grant this country a new opportunity to receive a love of the truth.

The Profit Motive

Daniel 7: 20 states concerning the little horn that his *"look was more stout than his fellows."* For a nation that started off so little and rustic as the U.S.A., it is quite amazing to consider today's prosperity relative to the rest of the world. To look at just one statistic, there is roughly one computer today for every four Americans; compared with one for every ten Germans, twelve

Japanese and 1,500 Chinese.[1] This abundance of good things, plenteousness at the table and a military strength that deters adversaries have produced a stoutness in America. Not to infer that America is overweight physically (although some are) but rather a stoutness of heart that fosters self-assuredness, self-reliance and not a little haughtiness.

Yet for all this, Americans are not satisfied. Henry Ford, one of the richest and most influential men of his day was asked what it was in all the world he really wanted now. His answer was - "just a few dollars more." Samuel Gompers, founder and president of the American Federation of Labor, led a movement that shook this country to its heels at the turn of the century. When asked just what it was that the Labor movement wanted in order to be satisfied, he replied with a one-word answer - "more!"

Ronald Reagan instituted what was called by some, "Reaganomics" in 1980. He believed if large cuts were made in the tax rates it would stimulate the economy by increasing profit margins and thereby opening avenues to full employment and prosperity. Reagan was right about his basic premise. Prosperity followed close on the heels of his controversial tax cuts. What he underestimated was **the element of human greed**.

When those who controlled the capital began to show substantial new profits, they didn't invest in new plants, machinery or in hiring new workers. Instead, with one accord corporate America began a massive leveraged

---

[1]Statistical Source: U.S. News & World Report, (2 May 1994), p. 46.

buy-out campaign. All the profits were poured into a junk-bond financed effort to swallow the whole world.

This take-over mania had two immediate results. The original stockholders gathered in a tremendous bonanza as take-overs drove stock prices through the roof. This created a cycle of greed. Secondly, the companies involved were acquiring huge debts that would have to be paid from future profits (or not at all).

For example, General Motors paid a great price to H. Ross Perot for his Electronic Data Systems, Inc. (EDS). Perot, who also found ways to get the government to pay him megabucks, became a multi-billionaire. General Motors, strapped by such an expenditure and even more so by the lifestyle that could fathom it, fell into a precipitous economic decline. G.M. fell from a fifty percent market share and nine figure profits to a thirty percent market share and nine figure losses. This goes on all across America. Everybody from the poorest illegal immigrant to the Rockefellers has their eyes on the goal of getting rich or richer.

There are plenty of good pious people who believe every lie the Reader's Digest (etc.) tells them. Congratulations! You are our next ten million dollar winner! (If...) The chances of being killed by lightening are a hundred times better than the chance of winning those millions. They are lured by the element of human greed.

"But they that will be rich fall into temptations and a snare, and into many foolish and hurtful lusts, which drown men in destruction and perdition. For the love of money is the root of all evil: which while some coveted after, they have

erred from the faith, and pierced themselves through with many sorrows." (II Timothy 6:9-10)

"The horseleach hath two daughters, crying give, give..." (Proverbs 30:15)

"Again the kingdom of heaven is like unto treasure hid in a field; the which when a man hath found, he hideth, and for joy thereof goeth and selleth all that he hath and buyeth that field." (Matthew 13:44)

"If therefore ye have not been faithful in the unrighteous mammon, who will commit to your trust the true riches? And if you have not been faithful in that which is another man's, who shall give you that which is your own?" (Luke 16:11-12).

What is the nature of true profit? What are the American people being fooled into accepting as a substitute? How do we get on the right road and stay there?

"Vanity of vanities, saith the preacher, vanity of vanities; all is vanity. What profit hath a man of all his labor which he taketh under the sun?" (Ecclesiastes 1:2-3)

There is no doubt that the American people are being bombarded with a deceitful message of monetary wealthiness. All the glitter and glamour of high-dollar society is being foisted on the American people as the culmination of success and the fulfillment of joy.

A profitable life is equated with financial success. Joy is portrayed as the high life. Having a good time means to be well-lubricated with liquor, admired and sought after by handsome members of the opposite sex and having a ball at one or another of the artificial meccas of instant gratification.

Now we realize that being rich in this world is more than just having money. Jesus said, *"Ye cannot serve God and mammon." (Matthew 6:24)*. Mammon is riches or wealth personified. We absolutely cannot afford to fall into the trap of serving wealth and riches (mammon). First, it excludes us from being able to serve God. Secondly, it is vanity. The end result is consumption. There is no lasting heritage or benefit to the soul from hedonistic and epicurean lifestyles. You can't take it with you. Thirdly, the quest for wealth will drown us in destruction and perdition. Remember the rich man and Lazarus. Fourthly and finally, you can never get enough. The horseleach hath two daughters, crying give, give. The horseleach is a pernicious blood-sucking pest which, even when removed, leaves a wound which will not readily heal.

The unbridled quest for wealth instigates in men and women an unscrupulous greed born of lustfulness. Once wealth becomes the goal, supplanting the desires and longings for closeness to God; a person will do things they ought not do. It's the love of money that corrupts the soul.

But Jesus likened the kingdom of heaven to a treasure which was hid in a field. When a certain man found the treasure, he hid it again, and for the joy of it, went and sold everything he had and bought the field so the treasure would rightfully be his.

A lot of people now-a-days don't operate under quite the same guidelines. people who are supposed to be good Christians borrow things and never return them. They just sort of assimilate ownership. There are a lot of supposed Christians who, finding the treasure, would have it home in a heartbeat. There wouldn't be any field-buying with them!

There are some who would steal to donate to God! One lady in the news lately was embezzling large sums of money from her employer and donating it to her church!

Jesus said if we can't be faithful in the unrighteous mammon, (there's no such thing as a holy dollar) then who is going to entrust the true riches to us? There is such a thing as true riches. If we intend to go to heaven, we had better upgrade our standards. It's a highway to heaven. We have to get up out of the mire and filthy lucre of this world so we can walk on that highway of holiness.

Moreover, He said if we have not been faithful in that which is another man's, then who is going to give us that which is our own? There are things - blessings and material benefits in this world which have been prepared for each of us. They are rightfully ours.

Let's take a carnal example. If all the land in the lower forty-eight states were to be evenly divided among all the citizenry, then every man woman and child in America would have ten acres to themselves. Yet some people are living in cardboard boxes on the most rat-infested streets of New York; way, way, way below their privileges.

Were we to inventory the contents of the average

bank vault, we might find a variety of things there. But we wouldn't find tomatoes, carrots and lettuce. These salad items are nice and they have their value, but it is not lasting value of the kind that is kept in bank vaults.

The same is true when we look to things of a spiritual nature. The material wealth (mammon) of this world is not permanent. It's only good for a few years here below and you can't take it with you. If we live this life to the absolute maximum, we might make it 120 years, but what is that compared to eternity with Jesus? - just the brush of an angel's wing. Gold is paving material in the City of God. Gemstones are used for foundation blocks. There are things much more valuable than these in the sight of God.

In I Peter 3:4 the Lord spoke concerning our ladies of the *"ornament of a meek and quiet spirit, which is in the sight of God of great price."*

> *"But where shall wisdom be found? And where is the place of understanding? Man knoweth not the price thereof; neither is it found in the land of the living ... It cannot be gotten for gold ... with the precious onyx or the sapphire ... No mention shall be made of coral or pearls: for the price of wisdom is above rubies ... Whence then cometh wisdom? and where is the place of understanding? ... God understandeth the way thereof, and He knoweth the place thereof ... And unto man He said, Behold the fear of the Lord,* **that is wisdom;** (Hallelujah!) *and to depart from evil is understanding." (Job 28:12-28, selected).*

Now we are beginning to see some of the things that

are truly profitable. Praise the Name of the Lord Jesus!

> *"Furthermore we have had fathers of our flesh which corrected us, and we gave them reverence; shall we not much rather be in subjection to the Father of spirits and live? For they verily for a few days chastened us after their own pleasure; but he for our profit, that we might be partakers of his holiness." (Hebrews 12:9-10)*

One more item of immensely great value we need to consider:

> *"Forasmuch as ye know that ye were not redeemed with corruptible things, as silver and gold, from your vain conversation received by tradition from your fathers; But with the **precious blood** of Christ, as of a lamb without blemish and without spot." (I Peter 1:18-19).*

So we see a few of the things that are truly valuable...

1. A meek and quiet spirit (among the ladies especially).
2. Wisdom (the fear of the Lord).
3. Understanding (to depart from evil).
4. The chastening and correction of the Lord.
5. The Precious Blood of Christ.

Fatigue

The saints of the Most high are being worn out. War is being waged against them. There are several aspects we need to check out.

First, we know from remembering the treatment America had given to the indians and negroes that the effects of this war with the saints is even more detrimental than slavery and subjugation. We are going past physical and spirit matters to speak of the destruction of men's souls. This is devilment of the first order and in this cause, he is definitely wearing a tux.

Second, we need to realize that this wearing out process is spiritual rather than natural in form. We can hardly say that American saints are worn out in a physical sense. Probably no more so than any other Americans. Most of us do not have an overly strenuous lifestyle. A forty hour work week is not so wearing when compared to perhaps ninety hours a week that great grandpa worked on the farm a hundred years ago.

Third, spiritually speaking and as a class (there are notable exceptions) American saints are already worn out (Bear with us.). The main ideas we want to think about here are **generative powers** and **spiritual response**.

By GENERATIVE POWERS, we mean the ability and propensity to give birth to new, powerful spiritual movements such as dimensions of praise, working of miracles, operation of the gifts and above all - the workings of the ministry.

An example would be - Paul and Silas in the Phillipian jail.

Here were two evangelists arrested for preaching Jesus. They were severely beaten and thrown into the innermost dungeon in an era when dungeons were awful to say the least. But at midnight, when they were in their darkest hour, they began to sing praises unto God and the prisoners heard them. They also got God's attention and an earthquake was generated which led to the saving of a great number of souls.

This is the kind of generative power that is needed and is lacking today. It is lacking because saints of the Most High are spiritually fatigued.

The second aspect is **SPIRITUAL RESPONSE**. By this we mean a reaction in a positive way to the voice and working of the Holy Ghost. An example would be Peter's hearing from God through a trance and being instructed by the Spirit to go with the three men sent by Cornelius. He responded in such a way that a great door to the gentile nations was opened for salvation and reception of the truth.

These two avenues are inter-related. Both involve the condition of the spirit of the saints.

In order to take the initiative (to use spiritually generated powers) we have to be living the **crucified life.** We have to be in that place where our spirits can rise above our circumstances to find opportunity in our pathway. We have to go past the level where we are listening to ourselves. We have to get to that place where our own needs can be set aside while we minister in another direction.

This is not easy to do. Our own voice and the needs of our flesh are loud in our ears. But the Voice we need to be hearing is still and small, soft and low; it's the Voice of our Savior's sweet love.

Spiritual response is what God is looking for. The Father *"seeketh"* those who will worship Him *"in spirit and in truth" (John 4:24).* The Lord is constantly seeking for people to do His will. Oftentimes He comes to us looking for that vital response to His approach.

In order to respond correctly in a spiritual manner we must have the prerequisite of **holiness**. The only way we can approach God, the only way we can hear and understand God, the only way we can respond properly to His initiatives is by living a life of holiness before Him.

It only takes the slightest bit of carnality to throw ourselves into a position where we are **incapable** of responding to the Spirit. Most of us have been there.

We can be spiritual enough to hear without being holy enough to respond. We can see an opportunity to win a soul to Christ but be unable to accomplish it. Usually the reason for such a condition lies in some avenue of carnality to which we have succumbed, perhaps only in the seemingly smallest way.

The problem in both spiritual response and the use of generative powers lies in the spirit of the society in which we live. We are constantly being bombarded with a carnal lifestyle from practically every direction. As we all know, every type of sin and moral looseness is being paraded in front of our eyes. People are walking around in public **without** most of their clothes and what little they are wearing is provocatively designed. The result is an instantaneous appeal to lust and carnal desire.

The news media is filled with all manner of sex, violence, gore, mayhem and just plain old wickedness. Anyone who picks up a paper, anyone in the course of daily life is going to view a great amount of all this. People are parading up and down the street filled in their minds and speech with all manner of foul cursing and degrading filthy language. This is an assault on the minds and souls of all who hear them.

The mores of great numbers of prominent people as well as everyday common people have totally collapsed. Society is hooked on an ever-increasing diet of smut and impurity. Crime, violence and rapaciousness are rampant and the criminals are going free.

We are being insensitized as a nation into a fog by the repetitive nature of these attacks. Like a battering ram before the gates of antiquity, we are being continuously pounded by this barrage. The sheer weight, intensity and frequency of these attacks wears down our ability to resist. Day in and day out, continually, continually we face the same kind of perspective and world outlook. If we were only once in a while faced with such opposition, it would probably be most offensive, but our resistance is being worn down.

When we become spiritually worn out we can forget about the reality of the cross and be **insensitized** to the **generative powers** of salvation and to the needed **response** to the will of God. This means we are unable to **affect our generation**. It means we can work and /or live next to someone for years, be saved ourselves, and never affect them.

This is not the will of God. We should pray for the will of God. For God is not willing that any should perish. If the will of God were to be thoroughly accomplished, no one at all would be lost. No one would go to hell except the devils. But when we find ourselves spiritually worn down and worn out, we are incapable of measuring up to God's will.

Anyone familiar with the works of the Holy Ghost on the foreign mission field should be able to relate to the American-ized nature of this problem. People overseas, especially in less developed countries are very hungry for God, never having had the opportunity they are having now. We hear continual reports of amazing happenings on the foreign field. We hear that God filled above

40,000 people with His Spirit at one rally in Ethiopia recently. Evangelist Billy Cole of Charleston, West Virginia, said, "God surpassed all of our expectations." Multiplied thousands have been filled with the Holy Ghost in other countries, including El Salvador, Guatemala, Korea, Papua New Guinea, etc. Amazing miracles and signs and wonders are taking place. Scores of folks are being raised from the dead.

Yet none of our preachers in America has anyone following around trying to get his shadow to pass over them. We have seen a measure of success but not the abundance. Why is all this going on abroad but not at home? Some doubt the veracity of the reports but that is faithlessness. Some of us are eye-witnesses to and participants in some of these events and therefore, we know them to be true.

The reason this is not happening at home is due to the worn out nature of the American saints. Oh, there is a smattering of vitality (compare the ministry of Christ Jesus Himself in His home town of Nazareth) but the need is much greater than the supply.

There is a great need for American saints to return to the roots of thankfulness. This is what got Paul and Silas started. We need to be thankful unto God for the salvation of our souls and for all that He has done, Jude said we need to *"earnestly contend for the faith that was once delivered unto the saints" (Jude 3).*

We are being opposed in our efforts by Satan and the legions of his devils. We need to recognize this oppression for what it is.

The United States Capitol

Chapter XII
Change

"For the times, they are a-changin'" Bob Dylan

Daniel 7:25, speaking of the little horn, says he shall *"think to change times and laws."*

Prior to the advent of the United States of America on the world scene in 1776, law was pretty much a static thing. There was a constancy to the laws of the lands. English law had been profoundly affected by the Magna Charta in 1215 A.D., but since that time, a span of 560 years, change had not been revolutionary in nature.

Rule in most nations of the world at that time was

invested in the person of the reigning monarch. Legislatures as such have existed since antiquity but have not been the focus of real power. Kings as a whole believed their powers were derived by divine right straight from heaven. This was generally true across the entire world from the emperor of China to the kings of England and France.

But the arrival of the United States on the world scene heralded an aura and era of change such as had never been seen before. The English parliament was no doubt a pattern of sorts for the American Congress and much of what came into being in America was based on English common law, but the world had never seen what the American system produced.

Today across America we find a tremendous in-depth legislative system that is producing one of the most startling innovations the world has ever seen; change for change's sake.

The House of Representatives and the Senate amounts to 535 persons, each of whom is armed with a staff of twenty or more aides and assistants, whose entire livelihood consists of writing new laws into existence. In addition to this, each of the fifty states has its own legislatures, house and senate, amounting to several thousand more lawmakers nationwide. These too are backed up by a formidable array of clerks and assistants. Add to all this the fact that each of the individual counties, cities and towns across America are "served" by their own town councils, county commissions or what have you. Then take into consideration the corporate boards of all the corporations, the student councils, teacher councils, the labor unions and whatever else have you across the country...

What we have is a tremendous system from top to bottom that is totally devoted to **change** of the status quo. There would be no need for all this if things were to remain the same. All these thousands and thousands of people are busily engaged, day in and day out, in changing the laws of the land. New laws and rules are constantly being added. Change is constantly taking place.

The change can be anything from the absurdly trivial to the audacity of an assault on the powers of heaven. One day there might be an official recognition of the new state insect. The next day might bring a law proscribing severe penalties for anyone who might stand up in opposition to one of the basic "freedoms" and "rights" of moral debauchery to which most of these legislative institutions have added their blessing. Never mind that the Savior Himself might stand up in opposition.

The crowning and overwhelming sense of urgency behind all of these legislative agendas is that of change; pure, basic and simple change. The American people have realized somehow (through the fog of everything they have opposed themselves with) that things are not right. So the answer the nation has come up with is change. Let's change things. What we have is somehow not working right, so let's change it.

Most people today have a realization and sense of urgency which tells them the American nation is headed in the wrong direction. This is nearly a universally held opinion. There may be a lot of varying thought about how to fix it, but nearly everyone can see the basic problem. The general consensus is; something has got to change, something has got to give.

We must remember that there is a wrongful spirit

operating behind the scenes in all of this. Remember that there is more to it than appearance. Two like-minded people can get together and do greater things (good or evil) than either one would do on their own. This principle works with spirits as well, whether it be team spirit, American spirit, or even the Holy Spirit for that matter. However, the things that are being produced by this behind the scenes working of wrongful spirits in America are to our detriment as saints of the living God. We need to realize that we are the **salt** of the **earth**. We are **changing** the world for God. We are in this world but not of it. We have to live here, but we don't have to conform and we don't have to be condemned with the world.

Let's remember that Daniel, as president over the 120 princes of Medo-Persia, was an upper-echelon member of the government of one of the four great "beasts" of gentile world power. Yet this did not make him evil. He also held great sway in the affairs of Babylon. Both of these countries were known masters of utter brutality, yet we don't see God blaming Daniel for it.

The spirit of a nation consists of more attributes than those of its principal citizens. Good and evil are based on how anything or anyone lines up with the Word of God. *"Let God be true but every man a liar." (Romans 3:4).* God had Esau pegged before he was born, before he had done anything! (See Romans 9:11-14). Manasseh, King of Judah, practiced unspeakable evil most of his life, yet he humbled himself and repented toward the end of his life and his prayer was heard by God, though the nation suffered for his crimes for years afterward (II Chronicles 33:1-9). So it is not a matter of looking on the outward appearance of things as a man does. God sees the heart.

God knows the end of a thing from the beginning.

Shall Think to Change Times

The times are constantly changing. America has taken thought to change times; not even content to let time run its course. A symbolic gesture in this direction is the institution of daylight saving time. The institutions of change have become so powerful in America that time itself has been assaulted.

Move the clock up an hour. Move the clock back an hour. Spring ahead and fall back. Legislate the date, move it around. Add leap day to the calendar. Scientists some time ago developed an atomic clock so precise that it is more accurate than the spinning of the world in telling time. They have to add leap-seconds every now and then to keep the clock tuned up with the world.

Albert Einstein was one of the most prodigious thinkers the world has ever known. The avenues of his thought processes were amazingly profound. His theories have propelled many scientists into enlarged areas of research that could change the very nature in which we live.

Einstein determined that if you could accelerate up to the speed of light, time would actually stand still. This theory has been proven even though nothing like the speed of light is currently attainable. This is because time is relative to speed.

Synchronized and identical atomic clocks, one left on earth and one shot into orbit have shown that, upon return of the orbiting clock to earth, time on that clock had slowed by a factor proportional to the rocket's speed and direction of flight.

Think, think, think! Of course all that's really been

done for the most part is to think about it. But that's what God said, *"shall **think** to change times."* Thinking has progressed too. People are thinking about time machines and ways to not only stop time, but also to reverse it.

This may seem to be futuristic lunacy but it has to be possible. It happened to Hezekiah's sundial. Consider the case of those men who were building the tower of Babel. When God confounded their language, He said, *"this they begin to do: and now nothing will be restrained from them, which they have imagined to do." (Genesis 10:6)*. So (God said) if people put their minds to do something, anything is possible.

Going one step further, we need to realize that God **is** light (I John 1:5). Therefore he must be operating at the speed of light. He can stop time in its tracks. No wonder His prophecies are so accurate. Our God operates independently of time!

Changing Laws

Contrary to the popular myth and mystique, there is no "illuminati" controlling the inner and behind the scenes workings of government and pulling all the right strings for their on-stage "puppets." To be sure, a lot of behind the scenes plotting and planning occurs. Many late and present influential persons, such as Walter Annenburg, J. Paul Getty, Armand Hammer and most of the ex-presidents have played the power broker and advisory role in the political process, sometimes without being in the limelight themselves. But at today's pace, change is happening so fast that there is no single interest group or personality that can get enough of a handle on the American political system to control it.

Things have gone past the place where change is occurring due to some national emergency. The change process is now so unbridled that change is taking place for the sake of change itself. In some of the high-technology fields such as computer science and communications, things are happening so fast that much of what is on the shelf is already obsolete.

In legal areas the change has been most sweeping. The law has been turned on its ear. We have already mentioned the issue of school prayer. Here the law has been reversed by the courts to prohibit prayer.

In another court case some years ago (Miranda) a confessed murderer was turned loose on society again, released to continue a career of crime because authorities had not "advised him of his rights" prior to taking his confession. This particular case marked the beginning of a national policy that has turned multiplied thousands of vicious career criminals loose on the streets again. The rationale has been that the police have to be perfect, while the imperfect criminal has the law on his side, working through every technicality.

Punishment as a viable entity has been removed from the legal lifestyle in America. People are no longer punished for their crimes. Rather, they are "rehabilitated." But rehabilitation does not solve the problem. Changing laws will not necessarily solve it either. A hundred thousand new police will not solve it. The only sure cure for the problem is a return to the ways of righteousness.

The trends we see in matters of the law are those of licentiousness. It has gone past liberality. It has gone past compassion and human kindness. In opening these artificial doors of criminality, the American nation is both making a statement and obtaining results. The results are compounding, gathering speed, hurtling downhill like a runaway train.

First, because injustice and evil are not being punished, there is a great resentment and hate building up in the nation. This hate is both on the part of the unpunished criminals and in society as a whole. Sooner or later, that hate is going to boil over. The boil-over will be tragic. Already we see some indications of this in the seemingly random, senseless and merciless nature of multiple murders increasing within society.

Secondly, there is a numbing sense of hopelessness which is a reaction to the licentiousness and the hate. This hopelessness is leading people into suicidal tendencies.

Thirdly, there is an increasing tendency to ignore and disobey the law. We can see it in even such a simple thing as speeding on the highways. There was a time when speeders were the exception; most people stayed fairly close to the speed limit. The exception now is the occasional driver who is within the limit. That driver is honked at, cursed, reviled and becomes a traffic hazard.

Make no mistake about it, there is a spirit at work here. It is a spirit which is bringing ruin to the American nation.

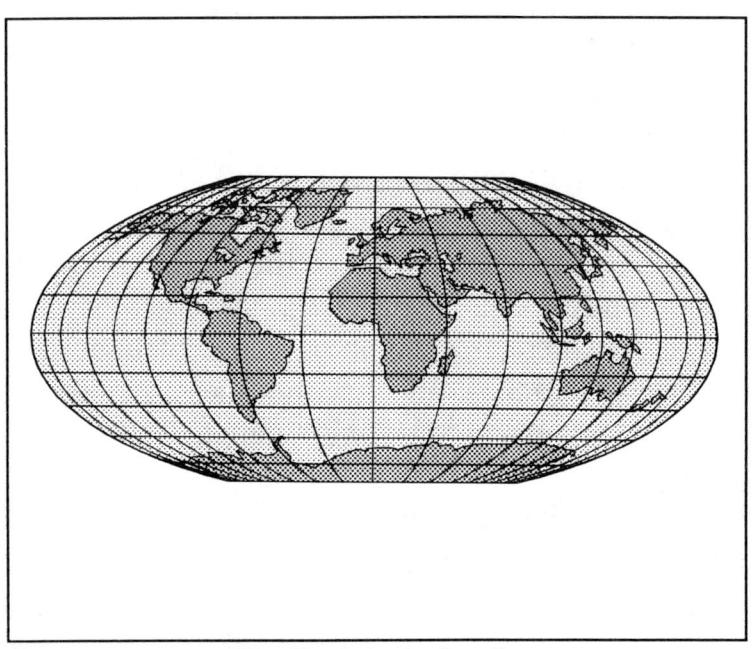

The Earth is the Lord's

Chapter XIII
The Ancient of Days
(When We All Get To Heaven)

There should be no lingering doubt in anyone's mind concerning the future fate of the kingdoms of this world. Every government, every nation, every kingdom is going to fall. The scriptures are very plain about this. Daniel 7:9-10 describes the process:

"I beheld till the thrones were cast down, and the Ancient of Days did sit, whose garment was white as snow, and the hair of his head like the

pure wool: his throne was like the fiery flame and his wheels as burning fire. A fiery stream issued and came forth from before him: thousand thousands ministered unto him, and ten thousand times ten thousand stood before him: the judgment was set and the books were opened."

This is a description of the Judgment Seat of Christ, before which all the saints will have to appear.

For those who are confused by the imagery here, remember there is only one God. *"One Lord, one faith, one baptism, one God and Father of all..." (Ephesians 4:5-6)* and *"one mediator between man and God, the man Christ Jesus" (I Timothy 2:5).* Jesus is not another God, *"God was in Christ, reconciling the world unto himself" (II Corinthians 5:19).*

This throne of judgment is separate and distinct from the "Great White Throne" Judgment of Revelation 20:11, which follows a thousand years later. The former judgment is reserved for those who are "Christ's" at His coming because the "last day" judgment "has no power" over them (Revelation 20:6). In contrast, the Great White Throne Judgment will be for the mass of humanity: all the dead - both small and great.

Daniel records millions (thousand thousands) ministering unto the Lord. This is speaking of those who have obtained through power and righteousness, the privilege and ability to serve the Lord Himself. This is an elite calling, not obtained by everyone. Ten thousand times ten thousand stood before Him (Daniel 7:10). This refers to the number of saved in the first resurrection, evidently on the order of 100 million souls.

We know this does not represent the White Throne

Judgment for two immediate reasons. First is chronology. The White Throne Judgment takes place **after** a thousand years of peace; after "tribulation" time, while this judgment takes place **prior** to it. Secondly, we know that current world population is on the order of five billion persons. It is incredible to think of, but some population experts assert that half of all the people who ever lived are alive right now. This is due to recent reductions in infant mortality and the dynamics of the population growth curve. At any rate, Daniel's number represents only a small percentage of the total world population: a number more in line with some estimates of spirit-filled believers.

So we know from this and many other references that God Himself is going to rule and reign in this world. The kingdoms of this world will fall and the government be turned to the saints of the Most High, who shall reign with Him on earth for a thousand years.

His Name is a great Name. The Name of Jesus is "Jehoshua," which means "Jehovah has become my Savior" or "Jehovah-Savior." It is an amazing thing that God Himself would come down from heaven and robe Himself in flesh to bring us salvation. *"To wit that God was in Christ, reconciling the world unto himself." (II Corinthians 5:19).*

His Name is to be magnified. To know Him is to begin to realize the greatness of what He has done. To see Him is to recognize that Christ Himself is the image of the invisible God (Colossians 1:15). When we begin to consider the magnitude of His creation; the stars and the vastness of space, this earth and all the living things in it, we then should recognize that the Creator is greater than His creation.

So we recognize the creation. We praise the Creator. We lift Him higher. Hallelujah! There is only one God! And there is one mediator between God and man, the man Christ Jesus (I Timothy 2:5). He is the Father in creation, the Son in redemption and the Holy Spirit in regeneration. He is Wonderful!

What a privilege to be a recipient of His mercy. May we ever be merciful to those who are around us, showing them the love and mercy of God. What shouting, what dancing and what joy awaits those who are His at His Coming. To what great lengths He has gone to save us!

The Times of Gentile Dominion are Coming to an End.

Chapter XIV
A Time, Times, and the Dividing of Times

Concerning the "little" horn, America: we have been examining his thought to change times and laws. Daniel 7:25 asserts that they shall be given into his hand until **a time and times and the dividing of time**.

This is indicative of the ascendancy and world power of the United States of America. The times and laws are given into his hand. The United States is exerting dominion in the world today. There is no other nation capable of wielding such power and influence. Russia has slipped and shown the world its inherent weaknesses. Europe is divided and incohesive (for now). China and all of the other nations are not capable of standing up to the economic and military might of the United States.

A good proof is in the United Nations organization. After World War I a similar plan was adopted and known as the League of Nations. The United States however, by a vote of the Senate, refused to join. Without the strategic strength and backing of the U.S., the League of Nations was weak and ineffective. In contrast however, with a home in the U.S., American financial aid and the assistance of American moral support, the U.N. has actually accomplished a few things. We must realize though, that there is no lasting peace without the Prince of Peace, Jesus Christ.

American power and dominion is evident throughout the world. Had the American nation been of a conquering mindset there is no doubt that the whole world would have knuckled under back when America was the only nation with atomic weapons. Had America been different, doubtless no one else would have been allowed to develop them.

Instead, what we see is world dominion. The United States is without question the temporal world leader in matters of economics, society, government and politics as well as in military matters. It is not a dictatorial dominion. The United States does not do much actual international dictating. Trend setting and word power are the two major methods of persuasion.

If there is a trend to be set in modern society, America will set it. The Americans did not invent or discover all the modern inventions - just the matters of electric lights, phonograph, telephone, radio, T.V., transistors, computers and a few dozen other major innovations. There is a power of inventiveness here. The whole world had access to the same raw materials, the same literature and research, the same tools and the same amount of time to use them all in; but it has been given to America to have power over these.

"Until a time and times and the dividing of time" (Daniel 7:25): This intriguing and mysterious phraseology occurs several times in prophetic scripture and bears examination. We could delve into the matters of days and months associated with these scriptures, but for our purposes here, it would be prudent to make three general notations.

First, Daniel 7:25 states that times and laws shall be given into the hand of the little horn UNTIL **a time and times and the dividing of time**. This refers to the dominion of the United States of America. Times and laws and world leadership in such things are given into the hands of the U.S. until this matter is fulfilled.

Second, we want to look at Daniel 12:7. This text covers a topic outside the immediate scope of this work. It is in reference to the time of tribulation known as "Jacob's Trouble." But in relation to our topic, we need to recognize the principles applicable here. This text states that the end of Jacob's Trouble, the end or the duration of these "wonders," will be for **a time, times and a half**.

Third, we find in Revelation 12:15 the discussion concerning the spiritual saga of the nation of Israel. We find the woman who represents Israel fled into the wilderness where she is hid and nourished for a period. That period is identified as being **a time, and times, and half a time**.

So therefore, we find a trilogy of applications here. The dominion of the little horn, the end of Jacob's

Trouble and the wilderness diaspora of Israel all culminate with this chronological event. We should look at it as a historical marking stone. This is an epic moment in history (Praise the Lord!).

It is a **time** for the nation of Israel, it is the **times** of the gentiles and it is the **dividing of time** for the kingdoms of our Lord and Savior. Israel will be moving out of the wilderness and into the limelight. God will sing the songs of Solomon's turtledove to Jerusalem. It is the voice of our Savior's sweet love.

Armies of redeemed men and the angels will come to fight for the remnant of the Jews who will have returned to Jehoshua their Savior. Legions of devils will flee in fright. Satan will be bound for a thousand years.

The time will have come for Jerusalem to be restored as the city of our solemnities. The remnant of the Jews will come from the four corners of the earth. Jesus Himself will rule and reign from Jerusalem for a thousand years of peace. **The times** of gentile world domination will have come to an end.

JESUS, WE WORSHIP YOU!

"Behold the Lord cometh with ten thousands of his saints!" (Jude 14).

From these times the Lord Himself will take the kingdom. It will be **the dividing of time** because the former ways will be things of the past. The old politics of spite and hatefulness will be gone. The nations will beat their swords into plowshares and they will study war no more. The whole earth will be restored to its former fruitfulness and will yield her strength in the harvests.

The wolf and the little lamb will lie down together and in all of the Lord's holy mountain, nothing shall hurt or destroy!

Because of the Words

There is an old children's chorus that goes like this:

> I'd rather be a little thing climbing up
> Than a big thing tumbling down
> I'd rather be a junior with a smile
> Than a grownup with a frown
> I'd rather be poor with a humble heart
> Than rich and lose my crown
> So, I'd rather be a little thing climbing up
> Than a big thing tumbling down.

King David of Israel, the giant killer, had a humble start in life. Just a shepherd boy, watching his father's little flock; but in that simple beginning he found joy in his God while tending the sheep. He learned to be a musician, evidently a good one as well, making good use of the hours at his disposal. He learned to communicate with God and to trust Him implicitly. He learned how to face down fear when a raging lion came up against him. David took hold of the lion by the beard and slew him! Absolutely amazing! A teenaged boy had learned confidence in God. Again, he killed a bear in a similar fashion. Yet all the while he was unknown, a young shepherd on a lonely hillside.

His first public job was as a delivery man. His dad sent him to deliver some food supplies to his brothers in the army. But Goliath, the Philistine giant, was troubling Israel. This giant, who stood about ten feet tall, had shoulders three feet wide. In full body armor and carrying a spear (Its head alone weighed twenty pounds!); Goliath had the entire Israelite army at bay. Every morning he would send out a challenge. "Send me out a man! We will fight! If he kills me, we will be your servants but if I kill him, you will be our servants. Send me out a man!"

No one was willing to fight the giant. They all feared the giant. They all probably hated the giant. Fear and hate are powerful emotions, but it is not enough to hate the enemy. Hate does not win battles. Every soldier has to learn to overcome fear. It is part of fighting. Some are overwhelmed with hate, but the only enemies who fall before fear and hate are the cowards and the helpless ones.

Strange as it may seem, **love** is the only emotion strong enough to empower the warrior to victory. *"For love is as strong as death." (Song of Solomon 8:6).* Love is the only thing that can look death in the eye and not come away defeated. Love is the only power that can make death blink. And God is love (I John 4:16). Somehow, if a warrior is going to fight and win, he has to have love as his motivating force. It can be love of life, country or family. Some may even love to fight!

David had developed a love of his God, his family, his country and a love of the armies of Israel. Goliath stood in direct hateful opposition to the things David loved. For Goliath, it was a fatal mistake. He was a champion, but he met the most powerful force he had ever faced that day. Goliath came face to face with love and it killed him.

David became an instant hero and an overnight success when he killed Goliath. Accolades and fame;

marrying the king's daughter; salary and the best society can offer were his. Nevertheless, it wasn't long before he faced another challenge. This time it was in the person of a jealous King Saul. Before long, David was fleeing for his life, away from wife, family, home and into the desert countries.

Is this the same David who fearlessly slew the lion, bear and Goliath the giant; now running for his life from the likes of King Saul?

Yes, indeed it was. In his love for God, David had developed a tremendous and over-riding respect for the man of God, the Word of God and the anointed leaders of God. He was already anointed himself but would not, under any circumstances, put forth his own hand to destroy the anointed man of God. It didn't matter what the circumstances were. Since Saul was the anointed of God, David was not going to touch him.

So, when Saul began trying to kill David by various means, he simply fled. David refused to do a wrongful thing - putting his hand forth to damage the Lord's anointed - no matter how much it cost him personally. And the cost was dear. His wife was given to another man. His family fled the country as fugitives and refugees. Yet David committed himself to the mercies of God.

This is commendable. It is one reason why God called David *"a man after his own heart"* (I Samuel 13:14).

So in God's time, David found himself promoted again within God's kingdom (Hallelujah!). Saul lay dead on a Philistine battlefield. David became the new king. What an honor. David himself knew he was anointed by God's prophet, Samuel, for this. But we can be sure he was not unimpressed by what came his way.

Promoted to top honor, David began to show another side of himself. Many kings, nobles and rich men in those days would take multiple wives to themselves, leaving poor men and others with no wife at all. David took full advantage.

David reigned as king seven years in Hebron. At that time there was a controversy involving Abner (the captain of murdered King Ishbosheth's army). David made a league with Abner, allowing him to abandon Ishbosheth and his followers. David accepted Abner's assistance in the expansion of his rule to cover all Israel on one condition; that his first wife, Michal, King Saul's daughter, be returned to him. So Abner took her from Phalti and gave her back to David, but their reunion was not a happy one.

Michal had born five sons to her second husband during the considerable years that had intervened. David took her five sons and had them hung to satisfy a grudge of the Gibeonites (II Samuel 21:8). This can't have done much to help his wife Michal or his marriage.

Before long David chanced to look out his window one day and saw a beautiful young woman taking a bath not far off. To make a long story short, he managed to get in trouble with her and to have her husband killed. For a man who had come so far and done so well, David had taken a mighty fall. It doesn't matter how well anyone starts out in life. Pride, carelessness and an inconsiderate attitude, together with lust can bring them down.

This long example has been brought out here to elaborately serve a simple point. The United States of America started off little in 1776 with an appeal to the providence of God. It was a simple nation built from the ground up by honest, humble people. Every government meeting in those days was started off with prayer. Many a cabinet minister spent time deliberating on his knees in prayer. President Abraham Lincoln said he was literally driven to his knees in prayer.

But somewhere down the road America left those simple beginnings. Somehow America has transmutated into a nation that is fast forgetting God. The nation that used to pray has forgotten how. It seems the best we can do anymore is a moment of silence. In an hour when the national problems are more profound than ever before, our leadership is messing up. We need to pray for them. We can see them messing up but that doesn't give us any excuse to trash the leadership of this nation. We are straightly instructed to pray for those in authority and not to speak evil of dignitaries.

The problem in this nation emanates not from the misdeeds and errors of the president, et al. The problem comes from a batch of devils wearing the American flag. The problem with both the leadership and the American people is that they are being deceived into following an evil pathway. It's time for somebody to get up and take a stand.

The story is told of an atheist (God be merciful) who went to a certain large high school to lecture the student body on the evils of organized religion and the foolishness inherent in trying to live for God, who didn't exist anyway. The atheist was well launched into this diatribe, haranguing all that was sacred, when a young girl stood up toward the rear of the auditorium and began to sing a hymn (reported to be "Stand up, stand up for Jesus, ye soldiers of the cross"). When she finished the chorus and started to repeat it, several more young people stood up with her and began to sing. Soon, more than a thousand were on their feet singing together.

One thing this nation definitely needs is for more people to get up and take a stand for Jesus. Never mind what people think and never mind the consequences. It will take more than braggadocio however. It will take holy living and that certain spiritual initiative coming from the life of a Spirit-filled individual.

This nation is headed down the wrong path. Daniel said,

"I beheld then because of the voice of the great words which the horn spake: I beheld even until the beast was slain, and his body destroyed, and given to the burning flame." (Daniel 7:11)

Without regard to the many problems the United States is beset with at home and the many sins this nation is guilty of; somehow the American nation and people think it our duty to moralize the conduct of every nation and people and society in the world.

If the Chinese nation (for example) doesn't necessarily believe every way we do about freedom of speech etc., the American nation seems to feel duty-bound to raise up a flag of protest, warning and condemnation. As the Chinese imprison, abuse and even kill their dissidents, Americans feel it is our job to correct them. Some politician will get up and condemn and harangue and perhaps even threaten. Americans don't stop to consider the consequences of their words.

American rhetoric inflames passions but does not solve the problem. The results are an entrenched leadership that has now learned to hate Americans; and the dead bodies of the dissidents stack up like cordwood. It has happened over and over again in the past, from Budapest (1956) to Tienanmen Square. One way or another, either for us or against us, we stir things up. It makes no difference whatsoever whether our observations are right or wrong. When we meddle in other people's business, we are building a legacy of anti-American anger around the world. We are missing the point, which is four-fold:

1. There is usually a real-life cause and effect for the things we don't like.
2. Who are we to judge when we are doing the same things or worse?
3. Foreign nations highly resent this judgmentalism.
4. This resentment is cumulative and will result in terrible consequences.

Libya is a case in point. When Khadafy and his supporters came to power in a coup, one of their first actions was to take over the foreign military bases (such as Wheeler AFB,) that had previously been permitted in that country. At the time, some of the hotheads in the U.S. wanted to take military action. What followed has been a long and fruitless escalating war of words. It escalated to the point that the Libyans (evidently) have terrorized Americans abroad and bombed an airliner out of the sky. Meanwhile the American Air Force has bombed an assortment of sites in Libya.

This sort of diplomacy is entirely counter-productive. All that is gained is increasing hatred and hostility. There were enough honest differences in the first place without manufacturing new hateful ones. (This is not to apologize for the Libyans or justify anything they may have done).

Americans should recognize foreign diplomacy for what it is: two-facedness. Furthermore, in this media-intensive age, journalists should not be allowed to conduct American foreign policy. Some of the problems Americans have gotten into abroad lately are the fault of television journalism. The eye of the television has no discretion and no conscience. The cameraman wielding it is being paid for one thing; action footage that will sell hard copy.

When the TV camera shows a starving Somali child it doesn't take into consideration that famine and pestilence are the consequences of sin, sent by God to punish and correct. Should we feed the hungry? Yes, of course, that is in our province. America is greatly blessed when it feeds the starving. Should we disannul the judgments of God? No, not in any way.

When Ethiopia was in a famine some years ago, factional fighting was preventing free American corn from reaching those who needed it most. At that time the proper American response was to take every available avenue to get food to the starving by some other means. The marines were not called in to meddle in someone else's strife.

He who *"meddleth with strife belonging not to him is like one that taketh a dog by the ears." (Proverbs 26:17)* When a vicious dog is taken by the ears, he will bite if let go and he will bite if held on to. An example would be the war in Vietnam. We had no business in Vietnam. It was not our quarrel. Once involved, we couldn't hold on and couldn't turn loose either.

So many politicians do not understand at all the proper use of the U.S. Marines. If, in fact, it was the case that we really needed to use the Marines in Vietnam, they should have been put ashore in Hanoi and Haiphong rather than in Cam Ranh Bay. Then they would have done their job and come home.

In the Ethiopian case, no Marines were called in. No helicopters were shot down. No American boys were killed and drug through the streets. Yet the hungry were fed. God's judgment was not disannulled. The political problems have been largely resolved. The country is experiencing Apostolic revival. The Christian church in Ethiopia today is seeing one of the largest percentage growths and total national revivals in world history.

These things have happened because somebody prayed. They have happened because television journalism was not permitted to run foreign policy. They happened because discretion is the better part of valor.

In Somalia on the other hand, things worsened instead of bettered. The Somalis were probably at least temporarily saved from starvation but the problem was definitely not solved. There is no prospect of national revival. An intense hatred and despising of America has been introduced where none existed before. Most importantly of all, thousands and perhaps millions of Somalis have had an open door to salvation slammed in their faces. By who and how is the gospel now going to be preached in Somalia? Where there may have previously been a door open for American missionaries (who have evangelized the globe) to preach the gospel unfettered in Somalia, that opportunity has gone a-glimmering.

Make no mistake. There is plenty of precedent for godly use of the institutions of national power. God used the Babylonian power to serve His purposes in the city-state of Tyre. God again used the Babylonians (who were evil in their own right) to punish the rebelliousness of Israel. There is no doubt in modern days that God used the United States to uproot and subdue the vicious Jew-hating Naziism of Adolf Hitler's Germany.

The powers that be are instruments and the *"minister of God, a revenger to execute wrath upon him that doeth evil." (Romans 13:4)*. There is no doubt that God uses national powers to execute His will. There is also no doubt that there are evil powers of darkness at work in the kingdoms of men. As we said before, there are evil spirits inspiring evil deeds in the collective that no individual would have ever concocted on his own. It is this evil collective thinking that stirs hatreds and starts wars.

Most of what the United States puts out today is rhetoric, pure and simple. But the words have an inflammatory effect and that effect is cumulative.

For the past several generations America has criss-crossed the globe with critical rhetoric. Can you remember the last time when America had much good to say about anybody? America has probably seriously lambasted every nationality and language that there is. Whenever the Americans show up, there is always criticism. Not enough this, too much that, this is wrong, so and so is dictatorial, inhumane, violates human rights. You are poor and unsophisticated. You are third-world material, undemocratic and ignorant.

We simply cannot treat people in other countries this way. People take offense. We can't go around the world cutting people to the bone with our words and expect to get by with it. Why does everybody have to measure up to America's yardstick?

Look at the body counts on American streets. Look at the homeless, the drug addicts, the criminals and the victims. This is the "dark side" of the American way.

If we as individuals were to go up and down our streets and begin to criticize our neighbors to their faces, what can we suppose the effect would be? We need to learn to leave well enough alone. If it's not broke, don't fix it.

Through the prophecy the Scripture says that because of the great words the horn is speaking, the beast will be destroyed and his body given to the burning flame. Because of this incessant American diatribe against everything and everybody, World War III is going to be launched.

What we need to be praying for right now is the extended mercies of God. God is a merciful God. Many times He has *"repented Himself"* of the evil He has already declared for particular individuals or nations. Consider the case of Jonah's mission to Ninevah.

Our ultimate faith and hope should not be rooted in the kingdoms of this world which are destined for destruction.

Chapter XV
Like unto a Leopard

"And I stood upon the sand of the sea, and saw a beast rise up out of the sea, having seven heads and ten horns, and upon his horns ten crowns, and upon his heads the name of blasphemy. And the beast which I saw was like unto a leopard, and his feet were as the feet of a bear, and his mouth was as the mouth of a lion..." (Revelation 13:1-2)

This beast is the post-Roman European Confederacy. It represents the latter day stages of Daniel's fourth beast. We notice at once that it is like a leopard. This is a reference to the institutions of democracy, which are rooted in ancient Greece. The Grecian empire was also likened unto a leopard (Daniel 7:6).

There are three references in Revelation to "seven heads and ten horns." These are Revelation 12:3; 13:1; and 17:3.

In Revelation 12:3 John saw *"another wonder in heaven; and behold a great red dragon, having seven heads and ten horns, and seven crowns upon his heads."* This dragon, also referred to as a serpent (Revelation 12:14-15), is none other than the devil himself, called Satan and Lucifer.

The seven heads and ten horns are manifestations of the devil in the earth. This is Satan's usurping effort to mimic the seven spirits of God as described in Revelation 1:4; 3:1; 4:5; and 5:6. Satan held at one time a pre-eminent position among the angels of heaven. He was the son of the morning (Isaiah 14:12) and the anointed cherub that covereth (Ezekiel 28:14); an angel of the highest order. But there came a time when pride entered into him and he became lifted up in his mind. His expression was, *"I will, I will, I will..."* He thought to be like the Most High; to sit in the sides of the north and receive the praises of the congregation. But his ambitious pride came to be his undoing and his downfall.

Satan is our enemy today. Though we may not have power to destroy him, we need not be defeated and deceived by his wiliness. God has given us a list of priorities by which we can defeat the devil every time. This scriptural priority list is as follows:

    1. Submit yourselves to God,

2. Resist the devil,
   3. And He will flee from you. (James 2:7)

We are instructed to put on the whole armor of God, including the shield of faith whereby we can quench all the fiery darts of the wicked (Ephesians 6:11-17). If we are properly attuned to God and committed to His will rather than our own, we shall have the upper hand in these matters.

In Revelation, chapter 13, we find one of the most studied, feared and discussed prophecy chapters in all of the Bible. These are the Scriptures relating to the "mark of the beast" and the mysterious number, "666." Again we find mention of seven heads and ten horns. John saw a beast rise up out of the sea having seven heads and ten horns and ten crowns on his horns. Rising up out of the sea is an indication that this beast comes up from the people themselves.

In that we have studied in depth the fourth beast of Daniel 7, we need to correlate the separate Biblical references to the beasts of this nature. A strong relationship exists between:
   1. Daniel's fourth beast (Daniel 7:7) which had ten horns;
   2. The great red dragon of Revelation 12;
   3. The beast out of the sea in Revelation 13; and
   4. The scarlet colored beast with seven heads and ten horns from Revelation 17:3.

1. Daniel's fourth beast; great and terrible, as we have previously shown, represents the Roman empire, both past and present, as the epitome of gentile world power. Daniel did not see the seven heads, which are ethnic manifestations. This is because Daniel's vision was the perspective of the Israelite nation. All gentiles are goyim to the Jew. There is no need to differentiate. Daniel did see, however, the ten horns. These are the national centers of political power as existent from antiquity, which have had great national impact on Jewishness throughout history.

2. The great red dragon, as we have explained, is Satan himself, as represented to the masses of mankind. This is the leviathan seen by Job (Job 41). The representation of Satan is two-fold. First, we see his duplicitous endeavor to duplicate the nature and the seven spirits of God. Second, we see Satan's kingdom in this world. Let us have no doubt about it. The politics, the wars, the murderous nature, the horror, the crime, the hate and the sinfulness and debauchery of this world are the fostered product of Satan. The seven heads etc., of the kingdoms of this world bear direct resemblance to the person of Satan himself because, as Jesus said to the Pharisees, *"ye are of your father the devil." (John 8:44)*.

3. The beast out of the sea (Revelation 13), represents the tribulation era embodiment of Daniel's fourth beast. This is the post-Roman European Confederacy we have mentioned so much previously. We see here the false prophet (as the lamb which speaks as a dragon) and the mark of the beast, which are the hallmarks of the tribulation time. This whole chapter gives us a ground-level view of both pre and post rapture pre-millenialism.

4. Revelation 17 describes a scarlet colored beast with seven heads and ten horns. But no crowns are seen.

Instead, John saw a woman sitting on the beast. This is mystery Babylon.

There are some people who come to the study of prophecy with pre-conceived notions and prejudices but leave behind the love, mercy and compassion of Christ. They follow after judgmentalism and vindictiveness. They hate sin and sinner alike. They are filled with passion of fleshliness and are greatly desirous to witness the wrath of God poured out on the inhabitants of this world. This is the same carnal attitude of those disciples who wanted to call fire down out of heaven (Luke 9:54) and were rebuked by the Lord.

Jesus instructed us to love our enemies instead of hating them. The Lord told us to turn the other cheek; to pray for them (not against them). We need to get a perspective on the overwhelming grief, sorrow and shame awaiting those who fall short of God's glory. Here is the patience and faith of the saints. We need to show compassion and love today!

The people of impatience and spitefulness have already concocted a number of prominent theories relative to "mystery, Babylon." But these theories are clouded by carnality. There is a time for everything. But the time for mystery Babylon is not yet.

* * * * * * *

There is no doubt about the accuracy of our observations relative to the ten horns and the American little horn. Daniel follows the chronology of these matters from his time right through tribulation into the kingdom age.

The theories that try to show some mysterious pause

in God's time table are incorrect. God's clock may not run fast enough to suit the carnal mind, but we are looking at things from this side of eternity. His clock never misses a beat. There is no disjointedness in Nebuchadnezzar's image until the stone cut out of the mountain strikes the image on its feet of clay.

We recognize that Daniel sees things from a different perspective than does John the Revelator or we today, for that matter. What we know for sure is that the written Word of God is true. We are filled with joy and thankfulness to our Savior when we realize that it is written for our benefit.

John sees the mouth speaking great things and blasphemies as a non-distinguished characteristic of the whole beast. He sees the whole beast as making war with the saints and overcoming them. These are not hard concepts when we consider the rapid pace of the times and the rate at which we see information, technology and culture transfers going on world wide. The European nations have taken a cue from the U.S.A. here. In historic respects they have done their own dirty work as far as the saints are concerned.

Power was given unto the beast over every nation and tongue. Right now we are living in an expansionary age when the power of the beast is being enlarged. It is becoming more pervasive and more invasive at the same time.

> "And all that dwell upon the earth shall worship him, whose names are not written in the book of life." (Revelation 13:8)

We ought to be very cautious about our worship and

the direction thereof. Knowledgeable men of God and pastors have been calling attention for some time now to the dangers inherent in what some are calling the "sports religion." Crowds at sports events are at record levels. Sports mania has caught hold as people go absolutely berserk in what amounts to a frenzied worship of the team, the game and the idolized heroes. We ought to be cautious about where we direct our worship.

* * * * * * *

"He that leadeth into captivity shall go into captivity: he that killeth with the sword must be killed with the sword. Here is the patience and faith of the saints." (Revelation 13:10)

There is a growing movement among a broad spectrum of Christians that physically opposes the abortion clinics and other institutions of evident iniquity. But we must be certain that we do not overstep the bounds of propriety here. We must be careful to love even our enemies. More importantly, we must strive to keep a right relationship to the law of the land. Those who rebel receive damnation to their souls (Romans 13:1-5).

It has become popular to physically oppose abortion clinics and the like, even with physical force and some have gone so far - inspired by a preacher - to commit acts of murder and mayhem against abortion providers.

This is wrong. If we do anything at all, it should be to pray for them (not against them). The government has raised the stakes in these cases by passing new legislation providing harsh criminal sentences against those who get caught up in these activities. The temptation to lash out against these things is certainly going to build as we see more and more of the wickedness of man. Here is the beginning of the patience and faith of the saints. If we are going to be saints, we are going to have to be patient. God will act in His own time.

> *"And I beheld another beast coming up out of the earth; and he had two horns like a lamb, and he spake as a dragon." (Revelation 13:11)*

This is the spirit of antichrist and the son of perdition.

In I Samuel 28:13 the witch of Endor, in calling up the spirits of the dead (necromancy) saw "gods" rising up out of the earth. This "beast" coming up out of the earth (Revelation 13:11) is a devil spirit. We are seeing many devil spirits being released from the bottomless pit where they have been shut up for eons of time. They are going forth to deceive and destroy the souls of the inhabitants of the earth.

Judas Iscariot is the one man in the entire Bible of whom it is written that it would be *"good for that man if he had never been born" (Mark 14:21)*. Jesus said of his twelve disciples, He had lost none except *"the son of perdition" (John 17:12)*. But there is more to Judas than just an evil man who went out and hanged himself. There is a spirit involved here. Remember that Satan entered into Judas (John 13:27).

Now Acts 1:25 states that when Judas by transgression fell, having committed suicide, he went *"to his own place."* This is a place prepared for him in the immediate underworld. And Paul, in referring to the coming of the Lord says;

> *"That day shall not come, except there come a falling away first, and that man of sin be revealed, the **son of perdition**; who opposeth and exalteth himself above all that is called God, or that is worshipped; so that he as God sitteth in the temple of God, showing himself that he is God." (II Thessalonians 2:3-4).*

So the spirit of Judas, which is the son of perdition, is all wrapped up in the personality of the antichrist, who looks like a lamb but speaks like a dragon (Revelation 13:11).

When this man is revealed, he will deceive. People will be fooled into actually thinking that this man is the manifestation of God. Many of the Jews will accept him as their messiah. (John 5:43). We might point out here that the "image" of the beast which John says the antichrist will cause people to worship, is actually the **representation** of the beast at large. People will worship a representation of the beast.

We are moving into a time of intense **spiritual** pressure, the likes of which have not been seen previously. The son of perdition is going to be immensely deceptive and spiritually powerful. He will have power to call fire down out of heaven and power to give actual life to the representation (image) of the beast. This is power enough to cause the masses who will be eye-witnesses of these things to cast aside their reservations and disbelief and submit to this man of sin their wills, obedience and worship.

We are entering into a time of **spiritual** pressure so intense that the devils are intimately aware of the (every) waking motion of the saints and ministers of God and are actively opposing them on every hand.

> *"And he causeth all, both small and great, rich and poor, free and bond, to receive a mark in their right hand, or in their foreheads:" (Revelation 13:16).*

This is the famous "mark of the beast." We **must** recognize that the key element here is one of **deception**. Satan is able to fool even ministers at times today. How much more when the spiritual guidance and check of the Holy Spirit is withdrawn? People are going to be deceived into taking this mark.

We are at the moment transitioning into a world atmosphere that transcends the monetary systems of the past. The pressures and the opportunistic pathway of the financial system have reached a doorway through which they will irresistibly be drawn.

On the one hand there are incredible numbers of financial transactions taking place with those who are already participants in the world banking systems. The checkbook system is undergoing radical change. Point-of-sale scanners are here. The whole banking world is lunging toward the electronic age where paper transactions are about as meaningful as a grocery receipt. The world is in transition.

On the other hand there are several billion people in the less-developed countries who are poised on the brink of entering the world financial market on a highly individualized basis. The sheer mass of number crunching involved would boggle the mind. But hardware systems currently available are up to it.

The translation of the Greek word for "mark" is possibly more accurately rendered "scratch" in English.

There is no doubt but that laser technology exists right now to microscopically "tattoo" a scannable mark, virtually invisible to the naked eye but readable by sophisticated scanning devices. To the recipient it would be scarcely more than a scratch.

This is not to say that we can pinpoint the actual mechanism of the "mark of the beast" but this is close to doing so. We can recognize the principle of deception here. The wiles of the devil will be at full force. People are going to be surprised and deceived by an expected enemy.

It is interesting to note at this time the nature of the so-called "Universal Product Code" or "UPC" which is currently the bedrock of the retail sales desk. We are not far from a day when nothing can be bought or sold without this numbering system printed on it. Currently it consists of two coded 5-digit numbers, with a sixth number either to the left or right side of it. It has been postulated by some that the mark of the beast will contain three six-digit numbers (666). Now we know that this is speculation. The realities of the actual mark and number of the beast are concealed until after the trumpet of God sounds.

The devil does not make a practice of openly soliciting people to go to hell and burn for eternity. He is deceptive; a liar and a murderer. He goes about to deceive people. He tells half-truths as well as utter falsehoods. He distracts attention from the true results. Then, when he gets someone isolated and in his power, he is a cold-blooded killer.

It is said that in order to enjoy the effects of modern theater, there must be a "willing suspension of disbelief" on the part of the audience. If that is true in the shadow industry, it is all the more true in matters related to the evil incorporate. Satan entices us to willingly unhinge our reservations. Once we have cut loose the anchors of our moral inhibitions, we are in the evil flow of Satan's currents. The current will carry us down to our destruction with no further effort on our part.

The whole key in all this is deception. Satan works to move us into a realm of false reality. Once we are living in Satan's false reality soap opera, the plot becomes immaterial. It doesn't matter what we do or what happens to us when the whole story line is a falsehood.

We ought to take time to re-examine the money end of this matter. The monetary system is currently the largest single problem facing our government. The governments around the globe are facing inflation, hyper-inflation, crime waves and budget crises of immense proportions. There is a much greater demand for services from government than there is a willingness to pay for them. All the tried and true remedies seem to be inadequate to solve these increasingly pressing problems.

As we previously noted, the governments in general are being irresistibly drawn through the doorway leading to total electronic accounting. We are headed for a cashless society. The benefits of such a system seem to be almost too good to be true from a social and governmental standpoint.

First, consider tax revenues. There is a tremendous amount of cheating going on relative to the IRS. For example, when the IRS began requiring the social security numbers of all dependents claimed on income tax returns, several million "children" mysteriously disappeared off the rolls.

There is a large number of transactions taking place

every day that should be taxed, but are not reported. Let's look at a few examples. Some employers have a practice of paying employees in cash "under the table." Both parties save by not paying the taxes required by law. It is a common practice for some merchants to under-report their sales transactions on both retail and wholesale levels to avoid paying taxes on them. We could go on and on.

Another area to consider is the tremendous amount of illegal activity taking place. Drug transactions are one prominent example. These drugs are illegal in the first place, but think of all the tax revenue that would be generated if these sales were taxed. The same is true of illegal gambling and racketeering. If all these items were taxed, there would be a tremendous increase in revenue generated for the government.

Second, the criminal aspect of many things would be exposed or eliminated by such a system. The IRS currently seizes property of drug kingpins and the like when their activities are uncovered. But in a cashless society, every transaction would be reported and there would be nowhere to hide these illegal dealings.

Third, theft and armed robberies would be reduced drastically by the institution of a cashless system. Can you imagine a robber sticking a gun in someone's face and demanding that some money (electronic variety) be added to his account? Obviously an electronic cashless society will put some serious clamps on the criminal lifestyle. Even electronic theft by embezzlement would be subject to control since every transaction could be identified permanently as to both source and recipient.

All these examples add up to compelling reasons why governments want to change to a cashless society.

Reports from employees of the government who work in the computer field indicate that many aspects of this system are already being implemented now.

Abraham Lincoln: The Great Emancipator.
This man's courage and the stroke of his pen set millions of people free. Yet he who the Son sets free is free indeed!

Chapter XVI
Freedom

Probably the greatest concept ever to emanate from these American shores is the concept of freedom.

The sovereign kings of the earth from the days of antiquity have always considered the people in their realm to be their **subjects**. People were subjected to the authority of the crown. But Americans have laid claim to the concept of freedom.

The opposite of freedom is imprisonment, slavery and servanthood. Those who are in prison are bound by walls and gates and chains. There is no physical opportunity for the prisoners for they are confined and limited to a concise area. They cannot come and go as they please. They cannot take action as they see fit. If they have a need, they cannot fill it. Their horizons are limited by the walls that surround them.

Prisoners are incarcerated because of the crimes they have been convicted of. Something in their past has caused the authorities to lock them up; to put them away where they can't cause trouble to society, where they can't influence the lives of anyone else. So prisoners are kept from freedom due to some fault of their own.

Slavery is an institution that is fortunately, nearly extinct in modern society. However, where it exists, slaves are also completely cut off from the concepts of liberty. They are completely under the control of another entity. Slaves cannot come and go as they wish, but are in bondage to a master who directs their activities. Their horizons are not so strictly controlled as a prisoner's, but their hope still looks through a small window into another world of freedom. Their life of bondage came through one of two venues; either they were sold as slaves or they were born into heredity slavery.

Servants are considered to be a cut above slaves. They are usually free in their person but bound for their labors to a master. Servants are usually either hired for their labor or have voluntarily let themselves into a contract of servitude.

In this land of liberty in which we live there are nevertheless great numbers of people who are prisoners, slaves, bound servants and hired men. We are not speaking of just the inhabitants of our jails and prisons. We are referring to the prisoners of Satan and slaves of sin; we speak of the hired servants of hell who toil so miserably in this life toward an eternity of doom and destruction.

Isaiah prophesied concerning the saved of the earth who from heaven's halls shall narrowly look at Satan lying in the pits of hell and say,

> *"Is this the man that made the earth to tremble, that did shake kingdoms; that made the world as a wilderness, and destroyed the cities thereof; that opened not the house of his prisoners?" (Isaiah 14:16-17)*

Satan does not let people go once he has them bound in shackles of sin. His prisoners, his slaves, his servants are morbidly attached to him and cannot escape. Their only hope is that somehow Jesus will pass by and come to their aid.

When Jesus came to Nazareth, He went into the synagogue on the Sabbath day and opened the book of Isaiah to read;

> *"The Spirit of the Lord is upon me, because he hath anointed me to preach the gospel to the poor; he hath sent me to heal the broken hearted,* **to preach deliverance to the captives**, *and recovering of sight to the blind,* **to set at liberty them that are bruised**, *to preach the acceptable year of the Lord." (Luke 4-18-19).*

There is an option available yet today. Jesus Christ stands in an open door. The hour of intercession is here. The hope of a life of freedom and productivity is set before the prisoners. There is an avenue of hope today.

The important aspect of all lives on this earth is the product of that life. This is the work or fruit that is produced as a result of living that life. A prisoner is shut up and is hard pressed to produce anything. All bound labor is for the benefit of someone else. Whether it is slave or servant, the results of their labor belong to others. These are the concepts of servile work. We thank God that Jesus Christ has set us free to live a productive life.

God Almighty does not view productivity in the light of our human standards. There was a dear lady who lived until 1991 in Fayetteville, North Carolina. She was blessed by God with reduced mental and physical capacity and spent most of her life in nursing homes, confined to a wheelchair and seemingly hopeless. Late in life she came under the care of a certain nursing assistant who was a caring Christian lady, filled with compassion. She managed to wangle a way to get our friend to the house of God, where Jesus marvelously filled her with His Spirit. Her life was changed. She became exuberantly filled with sunshine and joy. Through her enthusiasm, church services were initiated at the rest home where she spent the last (only one) year of her life bearing fruit for the Lord Jesus.

There is another concept that is transcendent in nature; the concept of fruitfulness. The scripture makes reference to a difference between works and fruit. In Galatians 5:19-25, Paul speaks of *"the works of the flesh"* and *"the fruit of the Spirit"* Fruitfulness surpasses works as much as the spiritual surpasses the carnal.

In concepts of fruitfulness we see a natural product of life. Even the scrawniest little apple tree will somehow manage to put out at least a few apples, no matter how small. It is not unusual for the tree to produce fruit, it is the natural product of life.

The goal of the Christian is to produce fruit. Spiritual fruit is the result of living a spiritually healthy life. The apple tree doesn't have to toil to produce apples. It soaks in the sunshine and drinks in the rain. It sends roots downward and lifts leaves upward. It spreads its blossoms out and fruit grows as a matter of course. This is all the design of God.

The purpose of the fruit is to make the seed attractive. The fruit is not the seed but it contains the seed. The apple tree produces the apple so someone will pick it and eat it and throw the core someplace where the seed can grow to produce a new tree.

The fruit enhances the prospect of the seed.

This nation was founded by a group of people who were without freedom in their native lands. the primary freedom they were interested in was religious freedom. They were looking for a place where they could be fruitful; where their fruitfulness would be undisturbed.

Now we need to realize in a spiritual sense, fruitfulness is the product of the Holy Spirit working in our lives. There is no amount of work that we can do that will produce fruit. On the contrary, the *"works of the flesh"* are destructive to the fruit. Jesus said,

"I am the vine, ye are the branches: He that

abideth in me, and I in him, the same bringeth forth much fruit; for without me ye can do nothing." (John 15:5).

This is exactly what we are longing for. This is the surge of joy in our lives that makes us productive. We want to bring forth much fruit. We want to have a great influence in our world.

Now the apple tree is not bettered by bearing much fruit. The tree sacrifices its fruit as an offering to enhance the prospect of the seed. It is the seed and the future generations of apple trees which will receive the benefit.

In our spiritual relationship with the Father we do not receive glory because we are fruitful. To God be all the glory. We are fruitful because His Spirit works through us. On our own we cannot be fruitful. It is the fruit of the Spirit. We as branches must **bear** the fruit.

Some years ago the author chanced upon a little apple tree that unbeknownst to him was in the last year of its life. A construction project was being planned that was going to require removal of that tree. But what fruitfulness! The branches were loaded down with apples to the point of breaking. It seemed there was no end to them. The last year of its life was undoubtedly the most fruitful it had ever seen. But when the construction workers came along and cut the little tree down to make room for progress, all of that fruitfulness was gone. There was a season of fruitfulness, but that season had come to an end.

There is a great and overwhelming need for American Christians to take these things to heart. We have long enjoyed the fruits of liberty in this land. We have been blessed with the freedom to worship God for so long that we have taken it for granted. But the time of taking things for granted has come to an end. The demonic enemies of freedom are slathering at the jaws over the opportunities at hand to put an end to spiritual liberty in the U.S.A.

We have to recognize that the judgments of God are true. There is a window of hope and opportunity for mercy. Nebuchadnezzar was instructed by Daniel to pray for a lengthening of his tranquility through the mercies of God. Yet there is no record that he ever prayed. Only one year after he received his warning, his prosperity came to a sudden end.

We **must** learn from his example. The moral crimes of the American nation are very great. Yet there remains a doorway of hope which we must strive to enter.

Jesus said, *"Ye are the salt of the earth" (Matthew 5:13)*. The purpose of salt is to flavor the food to which it is applied. Salt makes an otherwise bland and undesirable food taste better. It brings out the best flavors. **In sufficient quantities salt is also a preservative**. All types of meats can be "cured" with salt so that they will be preserved for a considerable length of time. No refrigeration or artificial methods are needed when sufficient salt is applied.

There is a great and pressing need for the preservation of freedom within the American nation. The salt needs to be applied so we can be *"unto God a sweet savor of Christ, in them that are saved, and in them that perish:" (II Corinthians 2:15)*.

Our generation needs to be reached for Christ and up to this point in time we have not been reaching it. Our purpose in savoring the world is to make it acceptable in the sight, smell and taste of God. By proper application of ourselves to those we meet in this world, we can flavor the world for God. We can put a flavoring into this world that will hold back the decay long enough that we can get our job done.

Our job is to bear the fruits of love, joy, peace. longsuffering, gentleness, goodness, faith, meekness and temperance in this world. By bearing righteous fruit in our environments, we will induce those around us to partake of the fruit. In partaking of the fruit, they will also receive the seed.

We recognize there are some folks, many folks who will never be saved. Our job is not to condemn. There will be condemnation enough on Judgment Day. Our job is to show forth the fruit to **everyone** so that we can be the true children of our Father.

There is more rejoicing among the angels in heaven over one repentant sinner than over ninety nine just persons who need no repentance (Luke 15:7). We have no realistic idea of the actual value of one soul saved from a devil's hell to become a recipient of the saving grace of Jesus Christ. It is past our comprehension.

A tremendous challenge lies before us. This world is lost and dying without God and without hope. Yet it is not the will of God that any should perish (II Peter 3:9). therefore, we should begin to pray as never before that the will of God would be done, both in our lives and in everyone we meet. We should take it upon ourselves to pray for the will of God to be done instead of our will.

We should realize by now that this nation is in serious trouble. Yea, rather, from all that we have already received from God there is no excuse for our not realizing that this nation is in deadly, serious trouble.

There should be no doubt in our minds concerning the future destructive war coming on the earth, tribulation and the **beginning** of sorrows.

Nuclear weapons have not been used in war since the United States detonated two small ones over the Japanese cities of Hiroshima and Nagasaki in 1945. Since that time there have been tremendous technological advances in the field of thermonuclear weaponry. Bombs are immensely more powerful, packaged in individually targetable clusters, deliverable by ICBM rockets, cruise missiles, planes, ships, cannons and even by backpack on an individual soldier.

In addition to this (sadly) there has been a tremendous proliferation of nuclear weaponry throughout the world. The United States, Great Britain and France all have substantial arsenals, the American stockpile being second to none. The Russians have an immense quantity of very large weapons together with modern delivery systems. The Chinese have substantial quantities of weapons and have recently developed ICBM rockets to deliver them. A number of the fragmented states of the former Soviet Union have nuclear stockpiles which rumor has it are available for sale to such nations as are willing to pay the price. It is reported that Iran has already paid the price and several others are negotiating. Israel most certainly has a number of bombs and the medium range missile capacity to deliver them.

It is strongly suspected that both Pakistan and North Korea have developed nuclear weapons. Iraq was caught trying to do so and may yet have at least partial capacity secreted away. South Africa, now with a national unity government of untested allegiance, has admitted to having developed at least five weapons; though it claims to have destroyed them. Japan recently purchased enough bomb-grade plutonium to build perhaps two hundred bombs. We could go on and on. The bomb is becoming more and more available while world tension and instability mounts.

The Scriptures give substantial insight into this matter. It is emphatically declared in several prophetic passages what is in store for this world. Zechariah 14:12 is one of the foremost examples;

> *"And this shall be the plague wherewith the Lord shall smite all the people that have fought against Jerusalem; Their flesh shall consume away while they stand upon their feet, and their eyes shall consume away in their holes, and their tongues shall consume away in their mouth."*

This is precisely a description of the medical trauma associated with direct radiation burns resulting from close proximity to nuclear explosions. Many of the Japanese victims in 1945 died this very type of horrible death. Zechariah associated this with the tribulation-era battles for the city of Jerusalem.

The modern disarmament movement's thinking is delusionary. Of all the weapons ever invented by man, there is no need to think that this one will be voluntarily done away with. Certainly the nations will attempt that and will think they have attained it. But,

> *"When they shall say, Peace and safety; then sudden destruction cometh upon them ... and they shall not escape." (I Thessalonians 5:3)*

We are not of them that fearfully look for coming destruction. We are looking for the return of our Lord and Savior, Jesus Christ. We are not here to predict the day and hour of His coming. We are simply looking and longing for it. We are believing the original message of the apostles and prophets. There is no substitute for the original message. We are built upon *"the foundation of the apostles and prophets, Jesus Christ himself being the chief cornerstone; (Ephesians 2:20).*

Since the apostles preached thorough repentance, we need to be preaching thorough repentance. It signifies the death of Christ. John the Baptist wouldn't baptize those who hadn't repented. This "raise your hand and repeat after me" stuff will not do. It is not found in the Scriptures. At one time God winked at ignorance but now commands *"all men everywhere to repent." (Acts 17:30).*

The apostles baptized all of their converts in water by immersion and in the Name of Jesus Christ. We need to do the same. Jesus said, *"he that believeth and is baptized shall be saved." (Mark 16:16).* Baptism is essential. Jesus would not have instituted it and commanded it if it were not essential. Peter said, *"Repent, and be baptized every one of you in the name of Jesus Christ for the remission of sins..." (Acts 2:38).*

We are familiar with remission of cancer and other dread diseases. Water baptism is for remission of sins. It is essential. It signifies the burial of Christ. We need to do it **in Jesus' Name**. Everywhere in the oldest sources it states that baptism took place in the Name of Jesus Christ. There is no substitute for the apostolic Scriptural way. To be baptized into Christ means to use the authority of His Name!

But Peter did not stop with baptism when he preached the inaugural sermon of the newly born church on the Day of Pentecost. Otherwise the world would have gotten along just fine on John the Baptist's message.

> *"Then Peter said unto them, repent and be baptized every one of you in the name of Jesus Christ for the remission of sins, and ye shall receive the gift of the Holy Ghost." (Acts 2:38)*

The Holy Spirit is the resurrection of Christ. The gospel is not complete without the resurrection. Jesus died. This is true. We need to be conformable unto His death through repentance. Jesus was buried. This is true. We need to be buried with Him by baptism. And then He arose. This is true. We also need to arise to walk with Him in newness of life.

There is nothing in the Scriptures which ever says that the outpouring and manifestation of the Spirit died with the apostles. On the contrary, this is the New Testament full gospel plan. It is the death, burial and resurrection of the Savior. This is the fulfillment of the Old Testament tabernacle plan of altar, laver and holy place. Furthermore, they all are types and shadows of the heavenlies.

The easy believism of many nominal Christians is insufficient. Simon the sorcerer *"believed and was baptized" (Acts 8:13-16)*, yet his experience was totally unsatisfactory. Peter said, *"Your money perish with you."* We should do everything we can to encourage full implementation of the gospel plan.

Does that mean we condemn those who have gotten no further than the altar? No, most of the Israelites got no further than the altar. The laver and holy place were for the priests only. But at Calvary Jesus opened up the way for all to enter the Holy of Holies through the rent veil of His Flesh. Ours is not a ministry of condemnation. We don't condemn or judge anyone. We preach the cross. To some it is foolishness. But to those who are saved it is the power of God.

We should *"earnestly contend for the faith"* in this hour (Jude 3). Jesus said, *"**Strive** to enter in at the strait gate: for many, I say unto you, will **seek** to enter in, and shall not be able." (Luke 13:24).*

U.S. Flag - 1777

Chapter XVII
More Amazing Faith

Prayer is an amazing thing.
Faith is even more amazing!

Some two thousand years ago Jesus spoke to His disciples about a certain sycamine tree and said:

"If ye had faith as a grain of mustard seed, ye might say unto this sycamine tree, Be thou plucked up by the root, and be thou planted in the sea, and it should obey you." (Luke 17:6)

This is an amazing concept, yet Jesus was not just speaking rhetorically here. The promise is really ours! He goes on:

> *"Which of you, having a servant plowing or feeding cattle, will say unto him by and by, when he is come in from the field, Go and sit down to meat? And will not rather say unto him, Make ready wherewith I may sup, gird thyself, and serve me, till I have eaten and drunken; and afterward thou shalt eat and drink?" (Luke 17:7-8).*

It is really the intention and will of God that we should have the things that we need. It really **is** the intention of God that we should witness the supernatural and be a partaker of the divine benefits. But first there is a requirement that we should tend to the needs of the Lord and His Body.

There is a precedent many times over in history for the prayer of one man or even one child to change the course of history for an entire nation. Daniel prayed (Daniel 9) for the sins of the nation of Israel pertaining to the prophecy of Jeremiah and the national period of captivity.

In all the quandaries and troubles that beset the United States of America, there remains a great and pressing need for prayer.

There can be absolutely no doubt about the verity of the Scriptures, warnings and promises of God. When God says that the nations that forget God shall be turned into hell (Psalm 9:17), it is as sure as the law of gravity.

This does not mean that God is cruel. For example, when an airliner crashes it is not God's fault. God does not necessarily cause it to crash, neither is He aloof and careless as to whether it crashes. There are finite laws of nature at work and there is a great need for application of wisdom to all things that we do. It is only when we violate the laws of nature or fail to use wisdom that we come crashing down.

God never told us to fly in airplanes. So, when we do we are taking the corresponding risks. If something or someone messes up, the whole thing can come crashing down. It is simply a most unfortunate application of the laws of nature. Whether it is airplanes, trains, cars, busses, sickness or any of the myriad ways we can come to grief, they all work the same way.

God cares. This we know. God does not want to see us come to grief. God sends out ample warning signs in every case of mortal danger we may face. The problem is - all too often - we are not listening.

Concerning a notable tragedy of His day, Jesus asked the question,

> *"Those eighteen upon whom the tower in Siloam fell, and slew them, think ye that they were sinners above all men that dwelt in Jerusalem? I tell you, Nay: but, except ye repent, ye shall all likewise perish."* *(Luke 13:4-5).*

There is an overwhelming need for repentance in the United States of America. We can understand that there are a lot of sinners who are not going to repent. There are wicked people in this nation who are willfully entwined in a downwardly spiraling progression of evil and they are not going to change their ways. They are fully and absolutely dedicated to an eternal destiny of destruction.

We have to grasp a greater concept here. We must seize the reality of God's sycamine tree promise. We can change the course of hell. God has empowered us to possess the gates of our enemies. God is looking for some one, some few; committed to saltiness, that will stand up in the gap for our times and our nation.

There is no doubt whatever concerning the great realities of prophecy, the nature of the "little horn" and the coming destruction of the kingdoms of this world. Judgment is coming. But why should it come before its time?

Why should a great host (and there is a great host) of bonafide saints of the Most High stand idly by while our nation, our communities and our dearest friends go down to an early and unwarranted doom? Why should we, who have the power on earth to move mountains, remit sins and change the course of nature, fail to take action in this, the doorway hour of our passion?

"The children of Ephraim, being armed, and carrying bows, turned back in the day of battle."
(Psalm 78:9)

There is no excuse for this. We cannot withdraw from the coming warfare to which we have already committed our souls.

"If thou has run with the footmen, and they have wearied thee, then how canst thou contend with horses? and if in the land of peace, wherein

thou trustedst, they wearied thee, then how wilt thou do in the swelling of Jordan?"
(Jeremiah 12:5)

The pace of the race is accelerating. We are moving into a time in which there are only two choices available to the people of God. Either we are going to throttle this thing up to run with the horsemen or we will slump back in slumber and be anesthetized into ineffectiveness.

This does not mean we have to wear ourselves out for Jesus. On the contrary, too many good people are doing that already. We have to pace ourselves and know when to push.

What we **can** do is to become **instruments of mercy** in this, our day of opportunity. God is not willing that any should perish, for His mercy endureth forever. However, unless His mercy is transmitted through the effectual work of intercession, then instead of mercy we will find calamity.

Consider the Scriptural example of Abraham as he pleaded with God for the salvation of Sodom and Gomorrah. He got God to agree to spare the city if only ten righteous souls could be found in it. What if he had persevered to ask for only three (the actual eventual number)? Would the Lord have acquiesced to an imploration for only three? God only knows. Nevertheless the principle is there for us to follow.

The administration of mercy can ameliorate and/or defer the judgment of God. Jesus judged the Syro-Phoenician woman to be a "dog" and therefore not worthy of the benefits of God. Yet she cried for mercy and begged for the dog's crumbs. She was abundantly rewarded for her persistence.

The time has come for the saints of God in these United States to begin to strive and seek for the mercies of God to be extended to this nation. We are instructed to pray for those in authority. We need to do it. We need to pray for our president and quit lambasting him. We need to pray for our senators, congressmen and especially for our diplomats and foreign service workers. We need to pray for military leaders, governors, state legislators, the sheriff and town councilmen. We need to pray that God would guide their administration. We need to pray that God would lead them to repentance. We need to pray like Daniel (Daniel 9) for the mercies of God on our people and our nation.

"...Turn unto the Lord your God: for he is gracious and merciful, slow to anger, and of great kindness, and repenteth him of the evil. Who knoweth if he will turn and repent, and leave a blessing behind him?..." (Joel 2:13-14)

In tribulation time, the judgment is certainly going to come. But let that judgment be upon the antichrist and the false prophet and their people, whose damnation is just. Let us instead believe God for a ministry of mercy and reconciliation and hope in these waning hours of our time.

The story is told by one of our missionaries to Africa, of some severe problems he was having with witchcraft. It seems that a group of local people were gathering on a nearby mountaintop for regular sessions of witchcraft, the results of which were greatly hindering the gospel and a deterrent to the salvation of many people.

One day, being fed up with this nonsense, the missionary began to pray to God to take that offending mountain and cast it into the sea. Shortly afterwards there began to be a flurry of commercial activity. Engineers and government officials began frequenting the area. Workers came in and constructed new railroad tracks into town and right up along the mountainside. Soon huge steam shovels appeared and, starting at the top, began to methodically scoop up that great big mountain and load it onto railroad cars for shipment down to the sea. There it was loaded onto ships and carried far away to a refinery. It seems that they had discovered that the entire mountain was made of iron ore!

There are no limits to what we can accomplish for Jesus in this hour if we will just believe.

> *"Therefore I say unto you, what things soever ye desire, when ye pray, believe that ye receive them, and ye shall have them." (Mark 11:24)*

Let us believe God for a revival of repentance in this nation.

Some two hundred years ago, Francis Scott Key stood watch at the bow of a ship in Baltimore harbor. A prisoner of the British, Key was compelled to watch a bombardment of his countrymen in Fort McHenry. The British navy brought the strength of their fire power to bear on that lone bastion of freedom. Key's friends and countrymen no doubt huddled beneath those walls of stone while the cannons roared. We know the words of the song Key was inspired to write that night...

> "...and the rocket's red glare
> The bombs bursting in air
> Gave proof through the night
> That our flag was still there..."

It is night time in America, a spiritual night, and the forces of darkness are all around us. We have never seen a spiritual onslaught of hell such as what we are witnessing at this very moment. The devil is filled with fury and has unleashed the foul powers of the darkest corners of hell. The enemy is coming in like a flood. Satan is foaming at the mouth at the prospect of bringing down the nation that has evangelized the world.

When evil men set off their fertilizer bomb beneath one of the twin towers of the World Trade building in New York, they were not trying to destroy a parking garage. Their intention was to bring that whole massive building, a skyscraper with thousands of innocent people inside, down into a shattered pile of glass and rubble. Be assured that in their next endeavor they will not use crude fertilizer. Knowledge has increased.

* * * * * * *

Who knows what winds of destiny were whispering to Francis Scott Key that night in 1814. From somewhere across the ethereal mists of time was a voice calling to him? Was he hearing something in the spirit that stirred his soul to pen those words? How could he know that two hundred years later it would be the rocket's red glare that would menace not just Fort McHenry, but all of this great nation? When could he have learned that massive nuclear bombs are detonated high in the air for maximum destructive effect?

We foolishly think that because Russia is economically prostrate that peace and safety have arrived. But every Russian rocket is still a menace. And what of the Chinese, and countless others who now possess the same technology? At what point will they feel it in their interest to pre-emptively strike; perhaps even anonymously unleash the forces of destruction? What of the haters of America who even now have come into possession of nuclear arsenals?

Will the sacrifices of our forbearers; just men of years gone by, be all for naught? Will the brave Americans who gave their lives to stop Hitler and his kind have suffered and sacrificed in vain? Will the times of America's righteousness be swept under a rug of indifference in this the hour of our greatest struggle? Will all the compassion, the feeding of the earth's hungry and starving children be wasted? Will America's love of the downtrodden go unrequited?

Are there not, even in this late hour, a few good men and women who will overcome materialism; who will stand up against the spirit of our age? By twos and by threes will we stand shoulder to shoulder and back to back to fight hell in the cause of liberty?

Francis Scott Key stood in the birthing hours of this nation's history and penned the words. He could not see the outcome, but could only feel the struggle; hence the anthem in the form of a question. It is a question he asked of us and our children. He looked for an answer from a people who were over history's horizon.

The Star Spangled Banner

Oh say can you see,
By the dawn's early light;
What so proudly we hailed,
At the twilight's last gleaming;
Whose broad stripes and bright stars,
Through the perilous night,
O'er the ramparts we watched,
Were so gallantly streaming.
And the rocket's red glare,
The bombs bursting in air,
Gave proof through the night,
That our flag was still there.
Oh say, does that
Star-spangled banner yet wave;
O'er the land of the free,
And the home of the brave?

The U. S. Flag ("Old Glory")

Epilogue

The time has come for us to rise to the occasion. Will we cling to the old rugged cross? Will we regain and retain our **spiritually generative powers**? Will we **respond** to the moving of the Spirit in this, our finest hour?

Bibliography

Adams, George B., The Growth of the French Nation, (Cincinnati, The Chautauqua-Century Press, 1896).

Breasted, James and James Robinson, History of Europe, (Boston, Ginn & Co., 1920).

Fox, Robin, The Search for Alexander, (Little, Brown & Co., 1980).

Urshan, Jonathan, The Times of the Gentiles, (St. Peters, MO, Tape Ministry).

Walker, Albert P., Essentials in English History, (N.Y., American Book Company, 1905).

American Destiny (The), (The Danbury Press, 1975).

Autobiography of Benjamin Franklin (The), (New York, Prestige Books, 1968).

Eerdman's Family Encyclopedia of the Bible, (1978 ed.).

Lincoln Library (The), (Frontier Press, 1953).

New Century Book of Facts (The), (Wheeling, Continental Publishing Company, 1962).

Scofield Reference Bible (The), (New York, Oxford University Press, 1945) King James Version.

Statistical Atlas of the United States, (U.S. Government Printing Office, 1914).

Thompson Chain Reference Bible (The), (Indianapolis, B. B. Kirkbride Bible Co., 1964) King James Version.

Works of Flavius Josephus (The), (Baker Book House, 1979), vol. 1.

CORRESPONDANCE

John R. Broyles
c/o Alpha Omega Press
154 Creekbend Dr.
Vass, NC 28394

ORDERING INFORMATION

Postal Orders: **Bro-Kin Productions**
19425 Indian
Redford Twp., MI 48240

Phone Orders: (313) 535-2271

Sales Tax: Please add 6% Sales Tax for books shipped to Michigan and North Carolina addresses.

Shipping: Book Rate: $2.00 for the first book and 75 cents for each additional book. (Surface mail may take 3 to 4 weeks.) Air Mail: $3.50 per book.

Payment: Check or Money Order, U.S. Funds.